# Voice for Non-Majors

Roberto Mancusi

ILLUSTRATIONS BY WESLEY CANADA

PEARSON
Prentice
Hall

Upper Saddle River, New Jersey 07458

Library of Congress Cataloging-in-Publication Data

Mancusi, Roberto.
 Voice for non-majors / Roberto Mancusi.
   p. cm.
 Includes bibliographical references and index.
 ISBN 0-13-231966-7 (alk. paper)
 1. Singing--Instruction and study. I. Title.
 MT820.M255 2008
 783'.043--dc22

                    2007051447

**Executive Editor:** Richard Carlin
**Editor in Chief:** Sarah Touborg
**Editorial Assistant:** Emma Gibbons
**Executive Marketing Manager:** Marissa Feliberty
**Senior Managing Editor:** Mary Rottino
**Production Liaison:** Fran Russello
**Permissions Specialist:** Kathleen Karcher
**Senior Operations Supervisor:** Brian Mackey
**Operations Specialist:** Cathleen Petersen
**Cover Design:** Studio Indigo
**Cover Image Credit:** Anthony Marsland/Stone/Getty Images, Inc.
**Manager, Cover Visual Research & Permissions:** Karen Sanatar
**Composition/Full-Service Project Management:** Teresa Christie, ICC Macmillan Inc.
**Printer/Binder:** Bind-Rite Graphics

Credits and acknowledgments borrowed from other sources and reproduced, with permission, in this textbook appear on
appropriate page within text.

Pearson Education LTD. London
Pearson Education Singapore, Pte. Ltd
Pearson Education, Canada, Ltd
Pearson Education–Japan
Pearson Education Australia PTY, Limited

Pearson Education North Asia Ltd
Pearson Educación de Mexico, S.A. de C.V.
Pearson Education Malaysia, Pte. Ltd
Pearson Education, Upper Saddle River, New Jersey

10 9 8 7 6 5 4 3 2 1

ISBN-(10): 0-13-231966-7

ISBN-(13): 978-0-13-231966-9

This book is dedicated to my wonderful wife, Staci,
and my three terrific children, Matthew, Daniel,
and Isabella.

# Contents

SONG ANTHOLOGY CONTENTS LIST     ix

PREFACE     xi

ACKNOWLEDGMENTS     xiii

ABOUT THE AUTHOR     xv

ABOUT THE PIANIST     xvii

**CHAPTER 1**    INTRODUCTION: WELCOME TO SINGING     1

**The Beginning**     1
**The Basics**     1
    Posture     2
    Listening to Yourself     3

**CHAPTER 2**    LEARNING A SONG: THE ABCs OF DO RE MI     4

**Learning the Music**     4
**Learning the Words**     5
**Putting It All Together**     6

**CHAPTER 3**    BREATH SUPPORT: FUELING THE VOICE     7

**The Respiratory System**     7
    The Diaphragm     7
    The Intercostal Muscles     8
    The Abdominal Muscles     8
**The Process of Breathing**     8
**Breath Support**     10
    Snake in the Grass     10
    Laughing Out Loud     10
    Picking Up a Piano     11
**Fueling Up**     11

**CHAPTER 4**    MORE THAN ANATOMY: THE INS AND OUTS
OF HOW WE SING     12

**The Parts of the Larynx**     12
    The Vocal Folds     12
    The Arytenoids     13
    The Cricoid Cartilage     14
    The Thyroid Cartilage     14

The Hyoid Bone                                                          14
The Epiglottis                                                         14
**Resonance**                                                          **14**
The Pharynx                                                            15
**Registers**                                                          **15**


**CHAPTER 5   VOCALIZING: IT'S NOT JUST A FANCY WORD   17**

**Basic Exercises**                                                    **17**
The Hum                                                                18
The Sigh-Slide                                                         18
The Siren-Slide                                                        18
Down the Stairs                                                        19
Up-and-Down the Stairs                                                 19
Skipping Up-and-Down the Stairs                                        19
**Advanced Exercises**                                                 **20**
The "No Jaw Tension" Hoedown                                           20
Head Register/Breath Support A-Go-Go                                   20
Buzz-Saw Blues                                                         21
**Sensational Vocalizing**                                             **21**


**CHAPTER 6   PRACTICING: A GOOD HABIT TO GET INTO   22**

**What Should You Do When You Practice?**                              **22**
**Where Should You Practice?**                                         **23**
**How Should You Practice?**                                           **24**
**How Long Should You Practice?**                                      **24**
**Make It Count**                                                      **25**


**CHAPTER 7   VOCAL TECHNIQUE: HOW WE USE WHAT
WE KNOW   26**

**Identifying a Good Technique**                                       **27**
What Are You Doing to Achieve the Sound?                               27
How Does It Feel Vocally?                                              27
Is Your Voice Tired after You Practice or Perform?                     27
Do You Feel Yourself Improving or Getting Worse over Time?             27
**Conclusion**                                                         **28**


**CHAPTER 8   REFINING THE SONG: PUTTING EVERYTHING
TOGETHER   29**

**Score Mapping**                                                      **30**
**Memorization**                                                       **31**
1. *Type:* Writing Repetition                                          31
2. *Type:* Verbal Repetition                                           32
3. *Type:* Cue Cards                                                   32
4. *Type:* Cumulative Method                                           32


**CHAPTER 9   PERFORMING A SONG: MORE THAN NOTES
ON A PAGE   33**

**The Painter's Palette and Vocal Colors**                             **33**
**Expressing the Text**                                                **34**
**The Eyes and Face: The True Gateway to Our Souls**                   **35**
Gestures                                                               35

**CHAPTER 10**   LIVING WITH YOUR VOICE: VOCAL DO'S
AND DON'TS                                    37

**Vocal Don'ts**                                            37
**Vocal Do's**                                              38


INTRODUCTION TO THE SONG ANTHOLOGY           **40**

THE SONGS                                    **41**

BIBLIOGRAPHY                                 **329**

GLOSSARY                                     **330**

INDEX                                        **332**

# Song Anthology Contents List

## Sacred Music

*Amazing Grace* (John Newton)
*Angels Through the Night* (arr. Philip Kern)
*Ave Maria* (High) (Franz Schubert)
*Ave Maria* (Low) (Franz Schubert)
*I Walked Today Where Jesus Walked*
    (Geoffrey O'Hara)
*The Lord Is My Shepherd* (Abraham Kaplan)
*Oy Hanukkah, Oy Hanukkah* (traditional)
*The Old Rugged Cross* (George Bennard)
*Star of the East* (Amanda Kennedy)
*When I Survey the Wondrous Cross* (Lowell Mason)

## Oldies but Goodies

*Beautiful Dreamer* (Stephen Foster)
*Because* (Guy d'Hardelot)
*Dixie* (Dan Emmett)
*Dreamy Hawaii* (F. W. Vandersloot)
*Jeanie with the Light Brown Hair* (Stephen Foster)
*The John Brown Song* (traditional)
*Leave Me with a Smile* (Chas. Koehler
    and Earl Burtnett)
*M-O-T-H-E-R: A Word That Means the World to Me*
    (Theodore Morse)
*Over There* (George M. Cohan)
*Smilin' Through* (Arthur A. Penn)
*Tenting on the Old Camp Ground* (Walter Kittredge)
*The Yankee Doodle Boy* (George M. Cohan)
*You're a Grand Old Flag* (George M. Cohan)

## Popular Music

*Have You Ever Really Loved a Woman?*
    (Michael Kamen)
*How Do I Live* (Diane Warren)
*Minnie, the Moocher* (Cab Calloway
    and Irving Mills)
*My Heart Will Go On* (James Horner)
*R-E-S-P-E-C-T* (Otis Redding)
*What a Wonderful World* (George David Weiss
    and Bob Thiele)
*You Are So Beautiful* (Billy Preston
    and Bruce Fisher)
*You Raise Me Up* (Brendan Graham
    and Rolf Løvland)

## Popular Stage Music

*Bring Him Home*, from *Les Misérables*
    (Claude-Michel Schönberg)
*Give My Regards to Broadway*, from *Little Johnny
    Jones* (George M. Cohan)
*Goodnight, My Someone*, from *The Music Man*
    (Meredith Wilson)
*I Cain't Say No*, from *Oklahoma* (Richard Rodgers
    and Oscar Hammerstein)
*If I Were a Rich Man*, from *Fiddler on the Roof*
    (Jerry Bach)
*The Impossible Dream*, from *Man of La Mancha*
    (Mitch Leigh)
*Johanna*, from *Sweeney Todd* (Stephen Sondheim)
*June Is Bustin' Out All Over*, from *Carousel*
    (Richard Rodgers and Oscar Hammerstein)
*Memory*, from *Cats* (Andrew Lloyd Webber)
*My Funny Valentine*, from *Babes in Arms*
    (Richard Rodgers and Lorenz Hart)
*On My Own*, from *Les Misérables*
    (Claude-Michel Schönberg)
*Over the Rainbow*, from *The Wizard of Oz*
    (Harold Arlen)
*Some Enchanted Evening*, from *South Pacific*
    (Richard Rodgers and Oscar Hammerstein)
*Someone to Watch Over Me*, from *Oh, Kay!*
    (George Gershwin)
*Summertime*, from *Porgy and Bess*
    (George Gershwin)
*We Need a Little Christmas*, from *Mame*
    (Jerry Harman)

## Classical Music/Art Songs

*Amarilli* (Giulio Caccini)
*Beauteous Night, O Night of Love*, from *The Tales
    of Hoffman* (Jacques Offenbach)
*Cradle Song* (High) (Johannes Brahms)
*Cradle Song* (Low) (Johannes Brahms)
*Der Vogelfänger bin ich ja*, from *Die Zauberflöte*
    (W. A. Mozart)
*Drink to Me Only* (Anonymous)
*Ein Ton* (Peter Cornelius)
*I Love Thee* (Ludwig van Beethoven)
*Le Violette* (Alessandro Scarlatti)

*Little Karen* (P. Heise)
*Matin Song* (Francesco Paolo Tosti)
*My Mother Loves Me Not* (High) (Johannes Brahms)
*My Mother Loves Me Not* (Low) (Johannes Brahms)
*Nina* (G. B. Pergolesi)
*None But the Lonely Heart* (High)
    (Piotr I. Tchaikovsky)
*None But the Lonely Heart* (Low)
    (Piotr I. Tchaikovsky)
*The Sea* (Edward A. MacDowell)
*Voi, che sapete,* from *Le Nozze di Figaro*
    (W. A. Mozart)

### International Songs

*The Ash Grove* (Wales) (traditional)
*The Fair Maid of Sorrento* (Italy) (folk song)

*Yo m'alegro de habèr sido* (Spain) (folk song)
*The Last Rose of Summer* (Ireland) (traditional)
*Loch Lomond* (Jacobite Air) (Scotland) (folk song)
*Cancion de Maja* (Spain) (traditional)
*O Tannenbaum* (Germany) (August Zarnock)
*A un niño ciegocito* (Spain) (folk song)

### Duets

*All I Ask of You,* from *Phantom of the Opera*
    (Andrew Lloyd Webber)
*Anything You Can Do,* from *Annie Get Your Gun*
    (Irving Berlin)
*People Will Say We're in Love,* from *Oklahoma!*
    (Richard Rodgers and Oscar Hammerstein)
*The Prayer* (David Foster and Carole Bayer Sager)
*Wunderbar,* from *Kiss Me, Kate* (Cole Porter)

# Preface

There are many class voice textbooks on the market today. Why write another one? When I first set out to write this book, I wanted to create a textbook that dealt with learning how to sing as it pertained to the students who made up the majority of my classes. Most of the students who have enrolled in my various voice classes have fallen into two distinct categories: (1) instrumental music majors who are taking the class simply to fulfill curriculum requirements; and (2) non-music majors who sing as a hobby or for their own enjoyment, and want to improve, but have no desire to pursue a career in music. I wanted a textbook that speaks to those students.

I have attempted to design a textbook that gives students the fundamental knowledge necessary to begin singing healthily, while trying to keep the presentation of that information light-hearted and accessible to all levels of musical background. I wanted to provide students with a solid "snapshot" of how to sing properly, as this may be the only exposure to voice instruction they will ever get. The information in this book is by no means exhaustive. The more advanced singer who reads this book will, no doubt, have many other things to add to this information. However, remember that this book is intended to give *non-voice students* and *non-musicians* a firm grasp of how to make sound safely and effectively, how to learn and memorize music, and how to convey that music once it is learned.

The other thing I tried to incorporate into the book is how the principles used in singing correctly can and should be used to *speak* correctly. The one common factor that most of us share is that we speak. By utilizing the principles of breath support and warming up, each person can dramatically strengthen the speaking voice as well. We are given only one voice; what we do with it is up to us.

# Acknowledgments

When I first began writing this book, it seemed like an overwhelming project. Only with the help of many people did this book become possible. I need to begin with my voice teachers. They have been my teachers and mentors, and are now my friends. Without their expert tutelage, this book would never have been possible. Dr. Anne DeLaunay and Mr. Eugene Cline (coach), you are both endless fountains of knowledge. Thank you for sharing some of that knowledge with me. I am honored to have had a chance to work with you both. Dr. Wayne Crannell, you were my first teacher and really helped me to find my way. Without your guidance, I'm not sure what I would be doing now.

For their help with this book, I want to thank Wesley Canada, for her illustrations (you have quite a career ahead of you); and Mrs. Laura Gayle Green and Ms. Debbie Keeton of the University of Missouri-Kansas City, for their assistance and time in helping to make sure that everything was in order. You are both dear friends and I thank you from the bottom of my heart.

Both myself and the publisher gratefully acknowledge the assistance of the following reviewers:

Marvin Latimer
University of Alabama

Peggy Sears
California State University, Bakersfield

Dr. Stephanie Tingler
University of Georgia

Because this is more than just a book, I would be remiss if I did not thank the following people for their help and assistance with the recordings. First, my thanks to Kayla Paulk: you are amazing. Your piano playing is superb and your insight into these songs was greatly appreciated. Next, thanks to Neil Rutland and Eastern New Mexico University, for their unending support and contribution to the supplemental recordings. I would also like to thank Brian Tapley, Kid Icarus Entertainment, Inc., and The Recording Den for mastering the recordings. The recordings turned out better than I could have imagined. Thank you for all your hard work.

Last, but certainly not least, I need to thank my wife and children for their constant support, love, and patience throughout this process. Also, special thanks to my wife for helping me with all the last-minute details of getting this book ready for the publication process. I am truly blessed to have such a wonderful family.

# About the Author

**Dr. Roberto Mancusi** joined the faculty of Eastern New Mexico University in the fall of 2004. He possesses a bass-baritone voice that has been described as "a glorious instrument . . . warm and very robust." Of the opera roles he has performed, his favorites are: Falstaff (*Falstaff*), Sarastro (*Die Zauberflöte*), Dulcamara (*L'Elisir d'Amore*), Dr. Bartolo (*Le Nozze di Figaro*), and Melchior (*Amahl and the Night Visitors*). In addition to operas, he has appeared as the bass soloist in such works as *Elijah* (Mendelssohn), *Messiah* (Handel), *Lord Nelson Mass* (Haydn), *Te Deum* (Dvorak), *Requiem* (Fauré), and *Carmina Burana* (Orff). He also made his first foray into musical theater as Prologus/Pseudolus in ENMU's 2005 production of *A Funny Thing Happened on the Way to the Forum*.

In addition to singing, Dr. Mancusi is an active clinician and adjudicator. He has given master classes for singers throughout the Southwest and Midwest. Dr. Mancusi holds a Bachelor of Music degree from Simpson College, and earned his Master of Music and Doctor of Musical Arts degrees from the University of Missouri-Kansas City Conservatory of Music. All his degrees are in vocal performance.

# About the Pianist

**Kayla Paulk** is vocal coach and accompanist at Eastern New Mexico University, where she coaches singers and accompanies students, faculty, guest artists, and choirs. Prior to coming to Eastern, she was a full-time accompanist and coach at the University of Oklahoma, where she collaborated with faculty, students, and guest artists in numerous lessons, master classes, and recitals. As a member of the Stetson University School of Music faculty in DeLand, Florida, from 1993 to 2003, she served as both Director of Accompanying and director of the Stetson Singers. Mrs. Paulk received a Bachelor of Music Education degree in piano from Stetson University and a Master of Music degree in accompanying and piano pedagogy from Florida State University. She has accompanied choirs in Carnegie Hall, China, Newfoundland, Norway, and throughout Europe; a highlight was her two seasons as accompanist for the Santa Fe Desert Chorale. Her work with operatic singers includes master classes with Marilyn Horne, Sherrill Milnes, Jennifer Larmore, Martina Arroyo, Marquita Lister, Leona Mitchell, and Maria Spacagna. The summers find her in Orlando, Florida, as a coach and accompanist for Metropolitan Opera baritone Sherrill Milnes's opera workshop, VOICExperience (http://www.voicexperiencefoundation.com). Mrs. Paulk recently served as national auditions pianist for Walt Disney World Entertainment.

# CHAPTER 1
# Introduction
## Welcome to Singing

So, you are taking a voice class. Sometimes it is called "Class Voice," or "Fundamentals of Voice," or simply "Voice for Non-Majors." Whatever the name, the class you are taking is designed to teach voice to a group of students at the same time rather than one-on-one. Whether you are taking this class because you like to sing and want to get better or you are taking it simply as a graduation requirement, this book is designed to boil down the basic building blocks of singing in a no-nonsense, straightforward way, without getting too technical. This book does not assume that you are going to pursue individual lessons or go into singing as a career, although it does not discourage either of those things. By covering topics from simple (such as learning a song) to complex (such as the anatomy of the larynx), this book presents the tools you will need to begin singing with good technique.

## THE BEGINNING

What kind of music do you like to sing? This seems like a simple question, but it is important for you to be able to answer it. If you are not singing music you enjoy, you will not commit yourself to what is necessary during your time in this class. Often students new to singing assume that any kind of voice training will result in them singing in a style they do not care for. They do not understand that the overall production of the voice remains the same even when the style or genre of music changes.

Think of singing like weight training. You need to learn the proper form for each exercise, the amount of weight you are initially able to lift, and the outcome you want to achieve. After you have all that information, you can then tailor your training to lift heavier weights and build strength, lift lighter weights and sculpt your body, or a combination of both. The muscles are the same; it just depends on how you choose to work them. This same idea applies to singing. Once you learn the proper way to support your sound, the art of vocalizing and practicing, and how to put it all together, you can apply the technique of singing to virtually any style of music. More importantly, you will be able to sing much longer in life, as good vocal production helps develop and maintain longevity in the voice.

Singing aside, how often do you talk? Sounds silly, doesn't it? But taking this class will help you with your speaking voice as well. How? By helping you utilize your breath support when you talk. Also, once you know the placement of the voice when you sing, you can tap this knowledge for use when you talk. This allows you to talk louder than normal without the fatigue and injury associated with screaming. This is because the volume comes from the support and vocal placement, *not* the throat. That is the key.

## THE BASICS

When you first begin to study something, you need to start with the basics. For singing, the basics relate to posture, listening to yourself, vocalizing, practicing, and making music.

1

Each of these contributes a great deal to the overall success of your voice. The last four items on that list are dealt with in later chapters. Here we want to deal with the first two.

## Posture

When we sing, we employ what some refer to as "singer's stance." This simply means standing with your feet about shoulder width apart, with one foot slightly in front of the other. Your shoulders should be back and down, with your rib cage expanded. Finally, your head should be held high, with your chin parallel to the floor (see Figure 1).

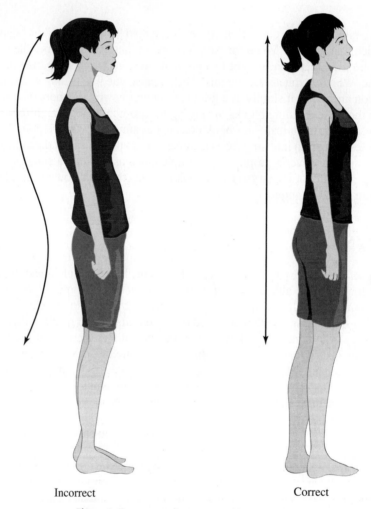

Incorrect                    Correct

**Figure 1** Correct standing posture: Singer's stance

The purpose of this "singer's stance" is to provide the best physical posture for breath support and space without overextending any part of the body. Although this is certainly not the only way to stand and sing, many teachers agree that it is the optimal way. Experiment with this posture. Put everything in the correct place as described here. Now, move a single, individual body part out of this alignment. Do you feel the difference? The correct posture for singing is a stable but flexible alignment of the body. One can stand still or walk without needing to adjust anything. The stance permits continuous maintenance of breath support. However, the moment you move just one body part out of that alignment, singing becomes much more work—work that is unnecessary. Let's face it, singing is work, but if you are struggling against yourself while attempting to sing, you are doing way too much. With a few minor adjustments to your posture, you will be ready to begin singing to your fullest potential.

## Listening to Yourself

How many times have you been singing only to stop suddenly because of what you heard? This is a normal occurrence for every singer, but it does represent a mind-set that needs to be changed when you begin to study singing. At this point, let's make a deal. It is important that you do not listen to your voice to make "quality" assessments. In this class, your teacher and your classmates will become your ears for that purpose. You may still listen to yourself to make sure that you are singing the correct notes; actually, that is a must. When it comes to what you think of your sound, though, you should begin to rely on the physical sensations you are feeling. As you begin to sing correctly, you will hear less and less of your voice in your head. Why? The reason is simple: The sound is getting out of your body. You are projecting your voice. You are utilizing the resonant space and the breath effectively, so the sound does not linger in your head. It is quickly going to the ears of your listeners.

With the sound moving out of your head, it stands to reason that you are not going to hear much of it yourself. So, how can you know what is good, healthy, correct singing? There are two ways. First, your teacher will tell you. He or she will become your external ears—the "ears of reason," if you will. The teacher's duty is to give you the feedback you need to correct any problems. Second, you can focus on the sensations you feel when you sing. Singing is all about physical sensations. We will discuss these sensations in more detail later on in the book. For now, just remember that those sensations, and the way they relate to the feedback from your teacher, will help you equate feelings with what is better, healthier singing.

So there you have it. Are you ready? You are about to begin the exploration of your own voice. You are in for some good times and some frustrating times. As long as you are willing to put the work into it, you will walk away from this class with a better understanding of how your voice works. You will also be making positive strides in your own vocal development, no matter what your original intent in taking this class.

# CHAPTER 2
# Learning a Song
## The ABCs of Do Re Mi

The process of learning a song is one of the most important things discussed in this book. Once you master the technical issues, you need to have a way of putting theory into practice. We do that by learning and singing songs. For some, learning a song is second nature. For others, it is as foreign and difficult as solving a calculus problem.

Let's start at the beginning. There are three steps to learning any song:

1. Learning the music
2. Learning the words
3. Putting everything together

By following these simple steps, the process of how to learn a song effectively and efficiently is demystified. Items you will need when learning a song include a piano/keyboard/computer (or a recording of the song), a tape recorder (or other device capable of recording), a regular pencil, and a red pencil.

## LEARNING THE MUSIC

What is it about a song that separates it from spoken dialogue? What separates musical theater and opera from plays? *The music.* Music is what differentiates singing from recitation. Because of that, the music is our first priority. When you first look at a song, you need to establish what you know about it. If you are able, you can begin by determining the key of the song, the meter, tempo, and rhythms. However, if this is your first time ever reading music, or if you are unfamiliar with a piano, you will need to find someone to help you with this step. After you have determined key and meter, you need to sit down at a piano or electronic keyboard and begin, *slowly,* to play the melody. *Note:* It is important to play as slowly as necessary to maintain proper rhythm throughout the song. Nothing is harder than unlearning a mistake after you have learned a song. If you have a recorder (tape or digital), now is the perfect time to use it. Tape yourself as you play the melody. This will give you a recording to practice with later. Play small sections at a time. Do not think you have to play through the entire song each time you go through it. As you repeat each section, gradually increase the tempo until you are at a speed you can use to practice the song.

Once you can play the melody, the next step is to sing the melody on a neutral vowel, such as "ah" or "aw." This begins the process of singing the song. Again, make sure that you proceed as slowly as necessary to avoid rhythmic mistakes. Do not sacrifice the integrity of the melody for a quicker practice time. After each time through the music, return to the beginning and gradually increase the tempo, until you approach the speed you will use when performing the song.

Now you will need the tape recorder again. If you have some basic, survival-level piano skills, you will already have completed the first step of this recording. If you have found someone to play for you, you will need them to record three things. First, you need the melody at performance tempo. Second, you need the melody with as much of the accompaniment as possible. Third, you need just the accompaniment. With those three things recorded, you are ready to finish the process of learning the music.

## LEARNING THE WORDS

With the exception of vocalises, every song has words. Each composer spent countless hours dealing with the text when he or she first composed the song. Usually, the natural inflection of the words is repeated in the musical rhythm. Stresses, accents, and other linguistic articulations are given or suggested by the melody. So, by learning the music first, it would seem that this step is almost finished as well . . . right? Unfortunately, that is only partially correct. As far as the flow of the words goes, you are nearing the finish line, but the language itself can be a tricky thing.

When you learn the words to a song, it is important to remember that these words are still in the context of a piece of music. Certain changes are made in each language to increase the ease of singing. For example, compared to languages like Italian, Spanish, and even British English, the American version of the English language is rather lazy. Much of what we say falls back into the throat and closes it to produce certain consonants. By moving the language more forward in the mouth and out of the throat, it is much easier to maintain the space needed to sing.

Here is an exercise to try:

Say the word "all" as you would normally say it. Did you feel your tongue pull back in your throat? That is not only unnecessary, but can be detrimental when you sing. Now say the same word, "all," but this time keep "ah" going in your throat, while the tip of your tongue comes up to the back of your top teeth to make the "l" sound. Wasn't that easier? That is how you *sing* the word "all." Now go back and forth between the two ways of saying "all." Do you feel the difference?

This is just one example of many that can be found in the American-English language. So, how do you combat the "laziness" of a language? By working for and maintaining a smooth, legato line.

A *legato* vocal line is a line in which all the notes of a certain phrase are connected into one continuous sound. This is done by singing through each note to the next without a break or pause in the sound. To accomplish this, we must sing from vowel to vowel in each word. This is successfully accomplished by another three-step process.

1. First, sing through the melody on a neutral vowel. This is the same thing you did when you first learned the music. Now, though, you are working at keeping each note of the given phrase connected to the following note.

2. When you have finished singing the melody on a neutral vowel, begin singing *just the vowels* of each word in the text. A solitary environment is a big help for this step, because you will probably feel silly singing these words without using the consonants. It is also not as easy as it seems. The idea is to maintain the same open and connected feeling that you achieved on "ah" with the vowels you will actually be singing.

3. Finally, add the consonants back into each word. These consonants need to be as quick and crisp as you can make them while still focusing on the vowel of each word. For consonants to be crisp and quick, you need to form them in the front of the mouth while maintaining the space in the back of the mouth. Remember this rule of thumb: Consonants are made using the lips, the teeth, and the *tip* of the tongue.

Only after you are able to sing the melody with the words are you ready for the final step in learning a song: putting it all together.

## PUTTING IT ALL TOGETHER

This step is the most fun and the most open to individual creativity. We discuss this step in depth in Chapter 8, but right now we cover the basics as they apply to learning a song. When you get to this step, you need to be concerned with how everything works together.

Has this ever happened to you or someone you know? You are working on a piece of music, either instrumental or vocal, that has a rather difficult last page. When you practice the final page by itself, it is not too bad. The high notes are attainable. The phrasing is fairly straightforward. The cadenza is challenging but not unmanageable. Then, you go to put the whole piece together. After you have gone through the entire song, the last page suddenly becomes your worst enemy. The high notes are impossible. The phrasing is inhuman. You would rather have a root canal than attempt that cadenza.

When you are learning how to pull all the aspects of a song together, you learn how to navigate the entire song. Chances are that there are some hidden problems in a specific passage or passages of the music that, alone, go undetected or unnoticed. When you attempt to sing through the entire song, though, those problems are compounded, and what was once an almost unnoticeable issue becomes a larger problem.

Only when you begin to view the song as a whole can true learning of the music take place. Until then, you are merely singing notes and words. This final step is the true art of singing. You will spend most of your practice time with this final step. It is important to remember that this step is to be attempted only after you have thoroughly completed the first two steps (learning the words and learning the music). Reversing the order of the steps or omitting a step leads to mistakes and problems that will then be harder to correct. These three steps, in this order, provide you with the necessary tools to succeed with any song you ever choose to look at.

# CHAPTER 3
# Breath Support
## Fueling the Voice

If you think about it, you have been breathing for as long as you can remember, right? Of course. All kidding aside, though: Are you aware that when you were a baby, you had the idea of breath support down cold? The way you used your breath was the epitome of efficiency. Babies really know what they are doing. Have you ever seen or heard a baby cry? Do they ever seem to get hoarse? Do they ever stop because they are vocally fatigued? Under normal circumstances, the answer to both of those questions is a resounding *no*. They will scream for hours as loudly as possible.

How can they do this? They naturally use their breath support. The next time you hear a baby cry—provided you know the parents—ask the parents if you can feel the baby's tummy. It will be rock hard. Babies may need us to do everything for them, but they do know how to ask for what they want *and be heard*. As we grow older, we forget many of those things we knew instinctively and, essentially, need to relearn everything from scratch. Now, as we are more cognizant of what we are doing to create sound, we need to discuss more of the intricacies of breathing, the nuts and bolts of what is moving and why.

## THE RESPIRATORY SYSTEM

We begin by taking a look at the pathway air takes as it travels from outside your body to your lungs. As you see in Figure 3.1, air enters the mouth or nose and proceeds to your trachea (TRAY-key-uh). From there, it moves into one of the main tubes leading to your lungs, called a *bronchus* (BRON-cuss), which in turn branches off into smaller tubes called *bronchioles* (BRON-key-oles) before the air finally gets to your lungs.

That is the pathway, but how does the air move into your lungs? We have to have some way to bring air from the outside into our lungs and then send unused air and waste gases out of our bodies. This is where an intricate system of muscles comes into play. Muscles in the chest and abdomen make the acts of inhalation and exhalation possible. There are three sets of muscles we need to look at: the diaphragm, the intercostal muscles, and the abdominal muscles. These three sets of muscles work in harmony to allow us to live from minute to minute. They do it without us thinking about it.

### The Diaphragm

The diaphragm (DIE-uh-fram) is the most important muscle involved in the breathing process. It is located at the bottom of the chest cavity, where it is attached to the rib cage and the spine. It separates the chest cavity from the abdominal cavity. In its relaxed state (after you exhale), the diaphragm is arched up. When it flexes (as you inhale), it moves down. This provides the room necessary for your lungs to fill with oxygen. It is important to realize that we do not have much, if any, ability to *voluntarily* control the diaphragm. We can control the conditions with which it begins the process of moving, but for the most part we cannot actually control the diaphragm, nor can we sense it directly.

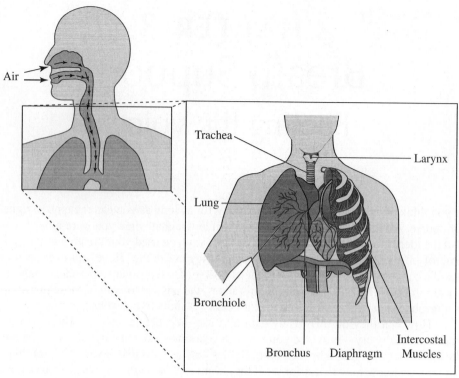

**Figure 3.1** The pathway of air

## The Intercostal Muscles

The intercostals are the muscles that are attached to the rib cage. These muscles work to expand and contract the ribs. There are two sets of intercostal muscles, the internal and external intercostals. Their names are derived from their location relative to the rib cage. The external intercostals are attached to the outside of the rib cage, whereas the internal intercostals are attached to the inside of the rib cage. Both sets of muscles are located between the actual ribs and are offset at roughly 90-degree angles from their counterparts (internal versus external). These muscles work against each other to allow the body to inhale and exhale properly. The external intercostal muscles elevate or expand the rib cage when you inhale. Because the ribs are bone and are connected to the rest of the skeletal system by cartilage, the amount of expansion is limited. The internal intercostal muscles compress or contract the rib cage when you exhale.

## The Abdominal Muscles

We all know about the abdominal muscles. These are the muscles targeted by the hundreds of exercise videos on the market today. These various groups of abdominal muscles, including, but not limited to, the rectus abdominus (WREK-tus ab-DOM-in-uhs) and internal and external oblique (oh-BLEEK) muscles, are used during the exhalation of air when breath support is engaged. Use of the abdominal muscles helps the main breathing apparatus return to its relaxed position (see Figure 3.2).

## THE PROCESS OF BREATHING

If you are reading this book, you know how to breathe. If you do not know how to breathe, you have worse problems than the sound quality of your voice. However, to

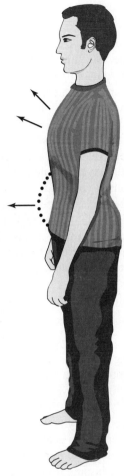

**Figure 3.2** Torso expansion when breathing

fully understand what *breath support* is, we must examine the specifics of how we breathe. What causes us to take air into our lungs? How do we get the carbon dioxide out of our bodies? Even more importantly, how can you make this process as efficient as possible?

To begin with, what causes air to come into our lungs? The simple answer is a vacuum. The absence or reduction of pressure in the chest, as the diaphragm descends into the abdomen, causes air to rush into the lungs. Think about a turkey baster. Squeezing the bulb of a turkey baster would be the equivalent of exhaling. Then, you stick the open end of the baster into the juices of a turkey and allow the expansion of the bulb to create a vacuum and suck up the juices into the utensil. That is what happens when you inhale. The diaphragm moves downward and the ribs expand outward and tilt slightly upward, which causes a vacuum in the chest cavity. This vacuum allows air to rush in from outside of your body to fill your lungs.

The process is reversed when you exhale. The diaphragm in its contracted state wants to return to its relaxed state. In doing so, the diaphragm moves upward into the chest cavity, which causes a decrease in the space available and squeezes the air and carbon dioxide out of the lungs.

That gives you a fundamental idea of how air moves to keep you alive. What we do beyond that to control the air flow constitutes breath support. When using the voice, we utilize breath support in an effort to make a natural process as efficient as possible.

## BREATH SUPPORT

Let's return to the turkey baster analogy. You have already filled the baster with juices and you are getting ready to baste your turkey. You can squeeze the bulb at any number of speeds depending on what you are trying to accomplish. You can squeeze it fast and make a big mess. Or you can use a nice, even, consistent flow that covers the entire turkey in the right amount of time with the right amount of juices. Which way do you think is best? Of course, the even, consistent method provides the best results. That is the same idea when it comes to breath support.

As mentioned before, when you inhale, the diaphragm moves down and your lungs fill with air. When you get ready to exhale, you use your abdominal muscles to fight the urge to let the air rush out of your body in one big whoosh. That resistance is *breath support*. Some students feel it as a squeezing-in or tightening of the abdominal muscles. Others feel it as a pushing-out against the abdominal wall. Either sensation is accurate. Experiment a bit to find which image comes closest to the sensation you feel, and which idea provides the best results in terms of control and consistency of air flow. Here are some exercises to help you with feeling the breath support engage beneath your singing.

### Snake in the Grass

You begin this exercise by taking a deep breath and hissing while exhaling. As you hiss, gradually get louder. Do you feel the resistance in your abdomen? That is the breath support. That is the most you will ever need. When you get to the extremes of your voice (i.e., extreme range, dynamics), that is how much support you will need. Throughout the remainder of your range, you will still feel that sensation, but slightly less. Remember, even and consistent is the goal.

Once you have hissed and felt the support engage, it is time to incorporate that sensation into the exercise. Start by hissing for three to five seconds, just long enough to consciously feel the support engage, and then proceed with an ascending and descending five-note pattern on a neutral vowel, like "ah" (see Figure 3.3).

**Figure 3.3** *Snake in the Grass*

With the completion of each pattern, move up or down the scale and repeat the pattern. You should begin to feel more in control of your voice. If you feel dizzy, you are straining and using too much effort. Back off the intensity a little and try again.

### Laughing Out Loud

Have you ever laughed so hard that your abdominal muscles hurt? That is the basis for this next exercise. It is not intended to make you double over in pain, but to help you feel those muscles working as you sing. Begin this exercise at a slow speed and gradually increase the speed in small increments at a time. As with the preceding exercise, move up and down the scale as you complete each pattern (see Figure 3.4).

**Figure 3.4** *Laughing Out Loud*

In addition to these two exercises, there is something you can do during any exercise that will help you with breath support. In fact, it takes your brain out of the equation. It tricks your body into doing what is necessary, without you having to think about it.

## Picking Up a Piano

Now, don't panic. You are not actually going to be lifting a piano off the ground. You *are* going to stand with your feet shoulder width apart, knees bent, hands under the piano. The important thing to remember is to keep your back straight as you do this. From this position, you are going to "lift" the piano until it is about to come off the floor. NO HIGHER. Do not really lift the piano off the ground. As you do this, sing any of the exercises mentioned in this book or any others that your teacher may have for you. Do you feel a difference?

What has happened is that your body, to continue to breathe during this strenuous activity, engaged the breath support automatically. You did not have to consciously engage the support. All you had to do was concentrate on the exercise that you were singing.

This exercise only works with large objects that you can "pick up" while maintaining good posture. The important thing to remember when doing this exercise is that most of the time, you will not have a piano to pick up while you are singing. Because of that, you need to use this exercise as a way of learning to feel the sensations of breath support; then practice to feel that same thing while you are standing upright and not picking up a piano.

## FUELING UP

Our voices are like vehicles. Both vehicles and our bodies need fuel to operate. For our bodies, air is the fuel. The breath support is our version of depressing the gas pedal on the car. The more consistent the flow of fuel, the more efficient the car can be. In our singing, we must always strive to keep a nice, even, consistent flow of fuel going so as to have the best and most consistent tone possible. With practice and constant vigilance, it is not just possible, but becomes a much easier thing to accomplish.

# CHAPTER 4
# More Than Anatomy
## The Ins and Outs
## of How We Sing

Now we need to direct our attention to that part of the physical instrument responsible for production of the primary vocal sound. As with any instrument, it is important to know what parts are used and when and how they work. If you do not know the ins and outs of the instrument you are studying, how can you expect to understand what your teacher is referring to during class discussions? Further, how can you begin to use that instrument as effectively and efficiently as possible? That is why we need to know exactly where the sound is made.

Production of sound with the voice (also called *phonation*) is done in the larynx (LAIR-inks). The larynx, or voice box, is located in the throat. As you know from our discussion of breath support, air enters the mouth and goes down the trachea. Located below the base of the tongue, but toward the top of the trachea, is the larynx. It consists of all the cartilage and membranes necessary to make sound. Let's take a look at its general makeup.

## THE PARTS OF THE LARYNX

The parts of the larynx we are going to talk about are the epiglottis (eh-pih-GLAH-tiss), the hyoid (HI-oeed) bone, the thyroid (THY-roeed) cartilage, the cricoid (CRY-koeed) cartilage, the arytenoids (a-RIH-ten-oeeds), and the vocal folds. These are the major elements of the larynx (see Figure 4.1). They all work in unison to create sounds. Let's start with the inside of the larynx and work our way out.

### The Vocal Folds

For a musical instrument to work, some part of the instrument has to vibrate. Whether it is the strings on a violin, the reeds on an oboe, or the membrane on a drum, each instrument has a vibrating part to create the sound. The same goes for the voice.

The vocal folds span the diameter of the trachea. When relaxed and open, they form the letter V, with the point of the V at the front of the throat. The location of that point is on the inside part of the thyroid cartilage and is what we call the Adam's apple. The vocal folds are attached at the front to the thyroid cartilage and at the back to the arytenoids. The folds come together to vibrate, producing sound (see Figure 4.2).

You can see how this works by blowing up a balloon and pinching it off. Then, stretch the edges of the balloon neck as far as you can while squeezing the balloon. Do you hear the sound the balloon makes? While you hear that noise, lengthen and shorten the balloon's neck. Do you hear how the pitch goes up and down? That is a simplified example of how your vocal folds work. The vocal folds come together initially to vibrate and create sound. As they are lengthened and shortened, they create

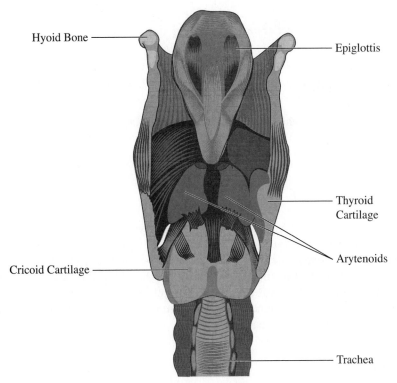

**Figure 4.1** Rear view of the larynx

different pitches. The movement of the vocal folds is based on the movement of the surrounding cartilage.

## The Arytenoids

As mentioned earlier, the vocal folds are attached in the back of the larynx to the arytenoids. The arytenoids are two pyramid-shaped cartilages located at the back of the larynx. They move in a number of directions; this movement lengthens or shortens the vocal folds and thereby creates small pitch changes. The muscles attached to the arytenoids and the cricoid cartilage are responsible for bringing the vocal folds together (a process called *adduction*) and separating them (a process called *abduction*).

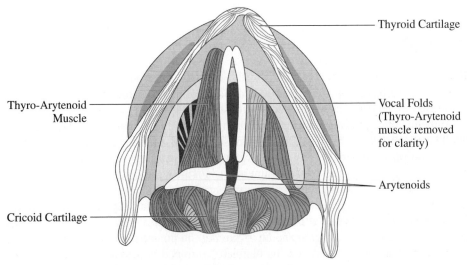

**Figure 4.2** The larynx from above

The easiest way to remember those two terms is to remember the first part of the each word. When you "add"-uct things, you bring them together. When you "abduct" something, you take it away.

## The Cricoid Cartilage

Located at the bottom of the larynx is the cricoid cartilage. It is the only cartilage that wraps completely around the larynx, and its largest point is located at the back of the larynx. It is the lowest part of the larynx.

## The Thyroid Cartilage

The thyroid cartilage is the biggest cartilage in the larynx. From the side it looks like a wide belt with a large belt buckle in the back of the larynx. Unlike a belt, the thyroid cartilage does not close in the back of the larynx. Instead, its two large horns, as they are called, are connected to the cricoid cartilage; they help the two cartilages rock together and apart, which makes the vocal folds get longer or shorter. This creates the large pitch changes in our sound. This is different from the arytenoids, which, you remember, cause more subtle changes in pitch.

## The Hyoid Bone

The hyoid is the only bone located in the larynx. It is shaped like the letter U or a horseshoe. It is positioned at the top of the larynx and is connected to the base of the tongue, as well as to other muscles.

## The Epiglottis

The epiglottis is located outside the top of the larynx, even though it is attached inside the larynx. Although it does not have a direct function in making sound, it is responsible for saving our lives every day. You see, the epiglottis has one main purpose. It closes over the opening of the trachea when we swallow so that no food or water can get into the lungs. Without the epiglottis, everything we swallow would first go into the trachea, because the esophagus—the tube that takes food and fluids to our stomachs—is located right behind the trachea.

## RESONANCE

Earlier, we compared the vocal folds to the reeds of an oboe. To continue with that analogy, there has to be something to amplify the sound, some sort of resonator or resonators. In an oboe, as with most wind instruments, that resonator is the end of the instrument, called the *bell*. It looks like a funnel on the end of a tube. For the voice, the "bell" is the mouth. When your mouth is mostly closed, the sound is muffled and soft. When you open your mouth by dropping your jaw, you create that same space you would find in the bell of a wind instrument, or in a megaphone.

You have seen a megaphone, have you not? It is what cheerleaders use to amplify their voices in large arenas and stadiums. The sound starts at the small end of the megaphone and leaves out of the larger end. If you think of your throat as the small end of the megaphone and your mouth as having the potential to be the larger end of the megaphone, you can see how humans are equipped with our own amplification source.

## The Pharynx

All instruments also have a tube or tubes that connect the vibrating source with the bell. The same goes for the voice. If you removed the nose and the mouth but left the space behind them, you would see the human equivalent of that instrumental tube. It is called the *pharynx* (FAIR-inks). It is the "highway" that moves the sound from your vocal folds to your mouth and out into space for everyone to hear. The pharynx is divided into three sections. Each section is named for the area it covers:

- Laryngopharynx—the space that encompasses the larynx, from the base of the cricoid cartilage to the base of the tongue.

- Oropharynx—the space from the base of the tongue to the roof of the mouth.

- Nasopharynx—the space from the roof of the mouth to the nasal cavity.

The pharynx and mouth are the main resonators of the voice. Adjustments made to these areas can dramatically increase or decrease the amount and quality of the sound a person makes. Beyond that, the nose and sinuses also provide some resonance to the voice. The sinus area located around the eyes and on either side of the nose is called the *mask*. Sensations and pressure can be felt there, especially when singing toward the upper end of the range of the voice.

## REGISTERS

Your first reaction to this section title may have been, "Price check on aisle 4," but we are not talking about cash registers. We are talking about the type of registers that exist in each voice throughout the span of the range. A general understanding of registers will help get you on the correct path to healthy vocal production and complete your understanding of how the voice works. In general, *vocal registers* are sets of vocal sounds that are similar to each other as a group, but differ from other sets of vocal sounds that are similar to each other within a different group. Sounds confusing, right? Think of registers this way: they are smaller sections of your overall range that create different physical sensations and are approached differently.

While the number of total registers and names of each register are debated among teachers (some use a one- or two-register method, while others simply debate the proper terminology), it is generally accepted that there are three registers in the voice: *chest* register, *middle* register, and *head* register. Sometimes these are called *voices* rather than registers, but the meaning stays the same.

It is important to realize that the sound for each register comes from the same place, the larynx. Just because it is called *chest* register does not mean the sound comes from there. The name of the register is more a description of the physical sensations you feel when singing in that area of your range. When you sing lower notes, you will be singing in your chest register, and it will feel like the sound is emanating from your chest. As you sing higher and higher in your range, it will feel like the sound moves up as well. It is no longer rumbling in your chest, but seems to be coming from a pressure that you may feel in your sinuses. It may also feel like the sound is shooting out of the top of your head. These are just sensations (not real physical occurrences), but they are the reason for the terminology of the upper register, called *head* register.

Then there is the *middle* register. The *middle* register is simply that: the register that occurs in the middle between the chest and head registers. It is an interesting area of the voice because so many factors play a part in the success or failure of notes placed there: factors such as what note(s) it is, what notes come before it, what notes come after it, how fast or slow you have to sing those notes, what the dynamic is, what vowel you are singing, what consonants are attached to that vowel, and so on. The list is quite long. With so many variables, it is easy to see why this is the area of the voice that students seem to dislike, especially when they first start singing.

The male voice also has an additional register, called *falsetto*. This register is easy to access in the voice. All a man has to do is "sound like a girl." The higher area of his voice that makes him pretend to sound like a female is his *falsetto*. For most men, this register is a weaker part of the voice that can be used to help find the upper head register. However, some men have been quite successful in training their voices to sing predominately in that part of their range, and have developed rather strong, resonant falsetto voices.

In a nutshell, that is your instrument and how it works. There are many other things in motion each time we make sound, but that is the basic nuts-and-bolts of it. The success of each voice depends solely on every part of your instrument working seamlessly with every other part. The same thing goes for speaking. Each part of the voice has its role in either creating the sound or enhancing the sound. Even the most recreational, amateur singer must know those basic parts of the vocal instrument if he or she is to maximize the efforts of sound production and, in particular, singing.

# CHAPTER 5
# Vocalizing
## It's Not Just a Fancy Word

*Vocalizing* is a fancy word for exercising the voice. We start through a series of musical exercises designed to get the voice moving and working. This is done at the beginning of each practice session. The purpose of vocalizing is the same as stretching and warming up before participating in a sport: to maximize performance, increase agility, and minimize the chances of injury. In this chapter, we explore the different exercises available and how to use them to achieve the vocal goals you and your teacher have set.

For our purposes, exercises can be divided into two separate categories: basic and advanced. Do not let their names fool you, though. They do not imply the level of development needed to do them. Instead, these names are meant to convey the level of intricacy within each exercise. Each type has its own usefulness and reason for being. However, it is important for you to practice both types of exercises. They complement each other. They are not meant to be exclusive of each other. Before we can discuss the exercises themselves, though, we need to describe the locales for proper vocalizing.

The locale for vocalizing will change as the purpose of the exercises changes. If you are vocalizing when you first wake, a terrific locale is the shower. Yes, everyone sings in the shower, but this is different. This is the time to get your voice ready for use throughout the day. The steam from the hot water acts as lubrication while you get your voice moving. Please avoid breaking into a rousing chorus of your favorite song right away! If you do some basic exercises when you wake, you will find that your voice is less tired at the end of the day.

If you are vocalizing as part of a larger practice session, you need to do so in a room with absolutely no distractions; a room with a mirror and a keyboard, if possible. This is necessary because you cannot focus on the exercises with a television playing in the background or, worse, a stereo playing other music. When you vocalize, you need to give your undivided attention to the exercises. If you do not, the benefits of each exercise are negated.

No matter what the reason for vocalizing, one rule must be followed at all times: *Do not vocalize in any position other than standing straight up.* (For more information on posture, see Chapter 1.) This means that you cannot vocalize in your favorite lounge chair, as you sit at your desk, or (some people's favorite choice) while you drive your car. These places rarely allow the proper posture necessary for good vocalizing. It is simple but true: just the act of standing up to practice begins to get your mind prepared for the task at hand. Once that simple step has been taken, the door for positive progress opens and you are ready to begin the exercises.

## BASIC EXERCISES

Basic exercises are exercises involving one vowel. They are not harmonically adventurous and are used primarily to get the voice moving at the beginning of each practice session. They stay within the first five notes of a key or within the tonic triad (major chord). In fact, some of the exercises do not use an actual pitch at all.

Additionally, these exercises are beneficial for use when you first wake up. Why warm up first thing in the morning? For the same reason, you let a car idle during the winter before driving it. The engine needs to warm up before it can run as smoothly as possible. If you start up your car and just drive away without letting the engine warm up, you will find yourself chugging down the street without much power until the engine eventually reaches the level of warmth necessary to allow safe operation. The same happens with the voice.

If you do not warm up your voice before you talk in the morning, your voice becomes like that engine in winter: chugging along until it gets sufficiently warmed up. Unfortunately, if the first thing on your schedule is a full day of classes with minimal talking, your voice does not get the chance to warm up sufficiently. Instead, it stays inactive, "chugging" throughout the day whenever you do need to talk. This is when some of the basic exercises, done first thing in the morning, become beneficial. Remember, though, these exercises are not limited to morning use. They can be used at the beginning of any practice session to get the voice ready for more intricate exercises. The exercises start small and build on each other, gradually preparing the voice for the work ahead.

So, what constitutes a basic exercise? Here are a few exercises for you to work with in your practice sessions. This list is not meant to be all-inclusive. Rather, it is intended as a starting point for other exercises.

## The Hum

Humming at a soft, relaxed level can be very beneficial early in the morning. No specific pitch is needed. Just begin by humming softly on any pitch and sustaining it. The next step is to do a little sliding around while you hum: first upward, then downward. Do not slide too far in any one direction. You want to keep the distance between notes pretty narrow. The idea is to begin to get the voice moving. The important thing to remember is to *slide* from note to note. This exercise is not for jumping around to different notes. That will come later.

## The Sigh-Slide

The next exercise utilizes many of the elements of the hum, except that you open your mouth. First, pick a note in the middle of your range and slide down, letting the voice "fall" slowly (see Figure 5.1). This should sound like a sigh. Each repetition of this exercise is done on higher and higher notes. Again, make sure not to go too high—yet. Movement of the voice is the aim. The other benefit of this exercise is that the breath really begins to get involved. Make sure you have begun to think about breath support as you journey higher and higher.

**Figure 5.1** *The Sigh-Slide*

## The Siren-Slide

We have all heard sirens outside as they go by our house or dormitory. This exercise is meant to mimic that sound. Begin on a lower note in your range. Follow it with a slide up about one octave and back down to the original note (see Figure 5.2). This can be repeated on different pitches, either higher or lower. When your voice begins to feel more flexible, you can expand the slide to encompass two octaves.

**Figure 5.2** *The Siren-Slide*

## Down the Stairs

This is the first exercise that utilizes actual pitches. The idea is the same as the sigh-slide, but, rather than sliding from each note, you sing each of the five descending pitches. Begin on a note in the lower middle part of your range. This note is the fifth note of the scale. From that note you descend to the first note of the scale (see Figure 5.3). This exercise is then repeated a half-step higher each time. As you approach the upper part of your range, begin moving back down with the exercise.

**Figure 5.3** *Down the Stairs*

During this exercise, be sure to maintain proper posture and support. Use a neutral vowel like "ah" or "aw" to keep the jaw dropped. It is also important to keep the tongue touching the bottom ridge of the mouth, where the teeth and gums meet. Do not let the tongue pull back in your mouth. The goal of this exercise is to begin warming up your entire range.

## Up-and-Down the Stairs

This exercise builds on the *Down the Stairs* vocalise. In this exercise, you are going to begin from below. Pick a pitch to begin with and move up five notes; then sing back down to the starting pitch (see Figure 5.4). Again, use a neutral vowel and maintain proper posture, support, and tongue position. The goal here is to maintain a smooth, legato line throughout the exercise. Make sure you are singing through the top note and returning to the low note, and not singing to or "at" the top note. Singing to the top notes results in a constricted sound on the upper tones and a large break in the range, because the voice is not able to support the size of singing without making certain adjustments. Keep the voice feeling high in the head and light throughout the exercise.

**Figure 5.4** *Up-and-Down the Stairs*

## Skipping Up-and-Down the Stairs

During this exercise, you expand the general idea of *Up-and-Down the Stairs* to encompass the entire octave. The idea is to sing 1-3-2-4-3-5-4-2-1. You outline the tonic triad (or major chord) of a given note (see Figure 5.5). Maintain a light, bouncy sound throughout the exercise. This will allow the voice to make the adjustments it needs to make as the range gets higher. Again, the goal of this exercise is to keep the line smooth and connected: connected to each note and connected to the breath.

**Figure 5.5** *Skipping Up-and-Down the Stairs*

## ADVANCED EXERCISES

Advanced exercises have an entirely different mission. These exercises are specifically designed to work certain areas of the voice, fix specific bad habits troubling a singer, or help the voice through a difficult passage of music. They involve more intricate vowel and word usage. They may also be more complicated harmonically and may be done at varying speeds. This is where the exercises get creative.

Be aware that, due to the difficulty of some of these exercises, they should not be used to warm up the voice. These are to be used only after the voice is warm and it is time to work on specific problems. It would be impossible to list all the exercises that fit in this category, as each teacher is constantly creating exercises based on the needs of each of their students. However, this small list gives examples of what constitutes advanced exercises.

### The "No Jaw Tension" Hoedown

This exercise is designed to help students who have problems with jaw tension when they sing. Whether it is their inability to open the mouth when they sing or a jaw that gets locked after they have opened it, this exercise will begin to get things loosened and opened up. Harmonically, it is the *Up-and-Down the Stairs* exercise from the preceding section (see Figure 5.6). The difference lies in the words used to sing this exercise. The following sequence is used for the ascending and descending pattern:

La-Bay-Da-Bay-Nee-Po-Too-La-Bay

The words are not the only part of this exercise, though. As the student begins to get familiar with this exercise, the speed gets faster. The combination of the words and the speed creates the conditions necessary for students to open their mouths and relax their jaws. It is quite difficult to lock the jaw and sing this exercise cleanly and accurately.

la - bay - da - bay - nee - po - too - la - bay

**Figure 5.6** *The "No Jaw Tension" Hoedown*

### Head Register/Breath Support A-Go-Go

This is a fun exercise if you are working the transition from register to register. It also works as a way to expand your breath support abilities. It is a simple ascending and descending scale with an added note (the 9th) on top (see Figure 5.7). However, at the pinnacle of the exercise, a bit of adjusting is done. As the voice approaches the 9th and descends, it does not immediately go all the way back down the scale. Instead, it uses a pattern 9-8-7-8-9. At first, the 9th should be hit three times, giving the final sequence of the exercise.

ah

**Figure 5.7** *Head Register/Breath Support A-Go-Go #1*

This allows the voice to make the turn over a break and begin smoothing that transition. If you would like to add to this exercise and work breath support, simply add more patterns at the top of the scale (see Figure 5.8). This exercise allows any amount of expansion. You will begin with three turns, but you can go to five, seven—whatever you and your teacher deem necessary.

oh _____

**Figure 5.8** *Head Register/Breath Support A-Go-Go #2*

## Buzz-Saw Blues

This is a fun exercise that is used to help develop the point, or focus, in the sound. It gets its name from the way the exercise begins. At its core, this exercise is the *Down the Stairs* vocalise, with one difference. This exercise uses the word "hing-ah" throughout. You start with the "hing" sound; really feel the buzzing it causes in the area around your nose and eyes (the mask). Then, drop your jaw to the "ah" while maintaining the same buzzing feeling you had at the beginning of the exercise (see Figure 5.9). The idea is to get the focus in the sound and then add the space. This is not an either/or exercise. It is also important to do this exercise in front of your teacher. It is very easy to add tension, especially on upper notes. Your teacher can work with you to eliminate the tension and make this exercise as effective as possible.

hing - ah _____       hing - ah _____

**Figure 5.9** *Buzz-Saw Blues*

## SENSATIONAL VOCALIZING

As you can see, vocalizing is not just important, but can be interesting and fun as well. Take the time you spend doing these exercises to really feel how your voice works. Feel the sensations involved with changes in register. Feel how the focus may make you want to sneeze when you first begin. All of these are important sensations. They are important because only when you consciously focus on what you are feeling are you able to recreate those sensations on your own in a practice room. When that happens, true progress can begin.

# CHAPTER 6
# Practicing
## A Good Habit to Get into

Practice . . . the word alone conjures up images of dullness and tedium. But, believe it or not, practice is the *only* way to achieve progress in anything. You cannot be a star athlete without countless hours of workouts, training, and *practice*. In fact, you have done very little throughout your life without practicing. Toddlers practice balancing and standing before they are able to walk across the room. The first few years of development are spent mimicking and practicing sounds before children begin talking their parents' ears off. Those steps, vitally necessary for the development of each child, are still forms of practicing. To master *any* skill, one needs to practice.

Before we can discuss how to practice, though, we need to clarify one simple point. You have heard both the words *practice* and *rehearsal*. What is the difference between the two?

In some circles, the words *practice* and *rehearsal* are synonymous. They are two words that achieve the same desired goal: a solid performance. However, further investigation reveals that they are two different things. Technically speaking, practice time is for working out the nuts and bolts of vocal technique, such as better breath support, wider range, and more vocal flexibility. Rehearsal deals with a particular song or songs and the repeated integration of the solutions worked out during practice. Cumulatively speaking, practice is done individually, whereas rehearsals are done with all the people involved (singer, pianist, any other instruments). Rehearsal includes the sum of all the parts of a performance. Practice deals with each of the individual parts, individually.

In this chapter, we will work with the cumulative description of practicing; that is, practice that is done by an individual rather than a group. We want to address what you should be doing in a practice session. Where should you be practicing? How you should practice? How long should you practice?

Before we can get into the logistics of practicing, we need to review one thing that can make practicing easier or more difficult: posture. Proper posture is extremely important to singing correctly. It allows you to maximize the amount of air you breathe in, as well as how effectively you use the air as you breathe out. Chapter 1 discussed "singer's stance." Do you remember what it was? You stand with your feet about shoulder width apart, one foot slightly in front of the other. Your shoulders are back and down and your rib cage is expanded. Your head is held high with your chin parallel to the floor. Work until you have this posture down solid. When you have achieved that, you are ready to begin practicing effectively.

## WHAT SHOULD YOU DO WHEN YOU PRACTICE?

Every aspect of singing should be practiced. Technical aspects like posture, breath support, mouth spacing, and vocal range should be addressed as your teacher requires them. Musical aspects such as pitches, rhythms, dynamics, articulations, and phrase shaping should also be practiced as they apply to each song.

The important thing to remember is to *have a plan*. Do not just go into your practice area and say, "Now, what should I practice today?" If you do that, your practicing will not be very beneficial. Have a plan. Decide beforehand what you are going to focus on during a specific practice session, and stick to your plan. This gives you a purpose for working. It focuses all your effort toward the achievement of that specific goal or goals. Focus allows progress to happen more quickly and easily. Also, the sense of accomplishment you gain upon completion of your individual practice goals will motivate you to practice again.

## WHERE SHOULD YOU PRACTICE?

It is always best to practice in a room designated specifically for practicing. Your school should have some rooms for that purpose. The reason a practice room is best is because it is quiet and has the larger items that you will need to "practice smart" and successfully (a piano and a mirror). If you do not have access to a designated practice room, you can use any number of different facilities where a piano or keyboard is available. If you are fortunate enough to have a piano or keyboard at your house, you may use that room, provided you can ensure that your practice time will remain uninterrupted. You might also check with your local place of worship to see if they have facilities you could use for the purposes of practicing.

Once you have found a suitable location for practicing, you will need to make sure you have all the supplies that you will need. Make sure you have a recording device of some kind, a couple of pencils (one regular and one red), and some water. Did you notice that a chair was not on the list of items that you need for practice? There are a couple of reasons for that. First, the piano/keyboard, more than likely, will have a bench that you can sit on. Second, and more importantly, when you practice you should stand up. Proper posture seems to be the first thing to go when people sit down. However, it is extremely hard to play your part on the piano, sing, and stand at the same time. Therefore, we need to address how to sit properly to maximize the breath support for singing. In Figure 6.1, you see a person sitting with correct posture. Do you see the way she is sitting up tall? Her spine is not rounded, nor is her chest collapsed. The torso is in the same position it would be in if she were standing. Her feet are flat on the floor.

**Figure 6.1** Correct sitting posture

This is how you properly sit in a chair when you are about to sing. The ribs are expanded and the diaphragm is able to fully descend to allow the most air intake upon inhalation. Seated like this, you can be confident that you are supporting the sound just as well as if you were standing up.

Here is a good way to make sure you are sitting correctly. Stand up straight using that "singer's stance" discussed earlier. Now sit directly down into a chair. Do not sit back; just sit down onto the chair. That is how you need to sit and sing. It feels quite different from what you are used to, doesn't it? That is all right. This will keep you from getting vocally tired from poor breath management. If you are a member of a choir, this is also the proper way to sit during rehearsal. Once everything is in place, you are ready to begin your practice session.

## HOW SHOULD YOU PRACTICE?

Learning how to practice correctly is as much of an art as is singing. If you do not practice the right way, you are wasting your time. When you first begin to practice, you must do so slowly. Trying to practice fast at the beginning will only create tension and bad habits that you will have to work twice as hard to break. Speed will come as you develop good practice habits.

As mentioned earlier, you should have a plan or goal for each practice session. That will determine how you should be practicing. If you go into a practice session without thinking about what you hope to achieve, how will you know when you are done? With a goal in your head, you will know how to go about accomplishing that goal. For example, if your goal is to learn the notes of a given song, then you know you will either need to plunk out the notes on a piano or have someone help you do so. If, however, your goal is to finish memorizing a song and get it ready to perform in class, you will not be spending as much time at the piano; you may find that you spend all your time working on expressions in front of a mirror.

Use your plan or goal to assist you with how (and what) to practice, but also remain a bit flexible. If you begin a practice session with the idea that you are going to work on expressions, but soon realize that there is still one passage of music that you have yet to sing correctly, change your goal for that practice session. You can either focus on the difficult passage or, if time permits, accomplish both goals. The choice is yours.

## HOW LONG SHOULD YOU PRACTICE?

The duration of each practice session has been debated among music teachers since the beginning of time. Should you practice one hour per day? Two hours? More? Is that amount of time all at once or cumulatively throughout the course of the day? How many days each week? As you can guess, it is possible to work yourself into quite an emotional state dealing with all these questions. Questions you should ask to help you determine the proper duration of each practice session, without getting an ulcer from the stress, include:

1. What do you want to accomplish during your practice session?

2. Do you have a performance coming up (either in class, church, or elsewhere) for which you have to have your music learned and ready?

3. How much time can you commit to practicing today and give it your *undivided* attention?

When you answer these questions honestly, you will find the answer to the length of each of your own practice sessions. This is not to say that a specific duration is wrong—on the contrary! If you want to set a goal of 45 minutes or an hour per day, terrific! That is a goal you can work toward. Voice majors regularly practice 1 to 1½ hours per day. This number may vary depending on other happenings during the day, but that is generally the amount of time for serious voice students. If you get to the 30-minute mark and you have not accomplished your original goal for that practice session, keep going until you complete that goal. Additionally, if you have a performance in class coming up, you may want to practice a bit longer to ensure that you are ready for your performance. You will be surprised at how much your nervousness lessens when you really know your song and want to share it, as opposed to having just barely finished learning it the night before you are supposed to sing it. However, if you find that you do not have enough time for a lengthy practice session, or your mind starts to wander after 30 minutes, then staying in the practice room for that extra time is a waste. You cease to be productive at that point. It is more important to practice smarter than to practice longer. You are only helping or hurting yourself.

## MAKE IT COUNT

Practicing is an absolute necessity for progress and vocal development. Whether you are just singing for class, or doing it as a hobby, you only get better with practice. Therefore, it is up to you to make sure that each time you practice, you are making that practice as efficient and beneficial as possible. No one has time to waste. Use your time to its fullest potential and you will be amazed by the results.

# CHAPTER 7
# Vocal Technique
## How We Use What We Know

Put simply, *technique* is the process you use to do what you do. In other words, if singing correctly is the destination, a good vocal technique is the route you use to get there. Whether you are involved in athletics and need to develop the proper technique to participate in the sport of your choice, or you play an instrument and need to develop a certain fingering technique to play your instrument, technique is essential to the progress and success of an activity. The same applies to singing. If you are taking this class as your only exposure to vocal training, use this chapter to assess when to ask for help. It is important to know when to ask for assistance, to avoid permanent damage to your voice.

The first step in developing a proper technique for singing (or any activity) is to gather as much knowledge as possible about the subject. With regard to singing, you have already learned about your instrument, how to develop proper breath support, and how to vocalize and practice properly. You know what is involved in making sound and which resonators enhance that sound. There is one other bit of knowledge that you need to be on your way to a healthy, proper vocal technique: *You need to be aware of your own voice.*

This sounds silly, but it is true. Teachers can only provide tools to help you with your instrument. We can hear different aspects of your voice and suggest exercises and music to assist with what we hear. However, always remember that it is *your* voice. You need to be constantly aware of physical sensations (both good and bad); points of tension, strain, and rigidity; and even when things feel terrific. All of that must be communicated to your teacher, who will be able to take that information and guide you in the right direction. This brings us to the next step in developing a proper, healthy vocal technique.

That next step is to *apply* what you have learned. With the help of your teacher, it is important to determine your strengths and weaknesses. This is something you cannot really determine on your own. Remember, you are not supposed to be listening to yourself. With your teacher's help, you will be able to adjust your technique to solidify your strong points and assist in developing your weaker areas. If you deal with only one aspect or the other, you will find that your strengths and weaknesses change places. Look at a weight lifter. Imagine a weight lifter who has incredibly strong arms but underdeveloped legs. That weight lifter spends the next three or four months working on nothing but leg exercises. Thereafter, his legs will be in terrific shape. However, neglecting his arms has caused them to get weaker. A good technique takes into consideration all aspects of a discipline without neglecting any part. By applying the information necessary for a good vocal technique, you begin to develop positive habits that you can carry with you no matter how you use your voice.

Aside from learning and developing the basics, another reason to develop a good technique is to expand your abilities. You may think that this is the same as dealing with your weaknesses, but there really is a difference. Let's say that every aspect of your voice is in place. Your voice is healthy, strong, and well maintained. However, you think you would like to expand your range, or you would like to sing songs that are a bit beyond your current abilities. These are not necessarily weaknesses, because you are already using your voice quite well. You just want to expand your abilities. If you have a firm foundation in healthy vocal technique, you, with the help of your teacher, can begin to explore those new and exciting facets of your instrument.

## IDENTIFYING A GOOD TECHNIQUE

By now, you are probably feeling overwhelmed by all of the information you have absorbed. You may be asking yourself, "How do I deal with this? How do I know if what I am doing is right or wrong? How do I know after this class if my technique is helping or hurting me?" The answers to these questions can be found by answering a few other questions.

### What Are You Doing to Achieve the Sound?

This question is easily answered. Basically, are you doing what your teacher suggested? Are you following the principles found in this book? If so, you are on the right track. If not, it is time to review the basics. It is always a good idea to periodically revisit the fundamentals of whatever you are doing. This keeps those basic ideas fresh in your mind. It also helps to head off any bad habits before they become too entrenched in your mind.

### How Does It Feel Vocally?

If you are singing correctly, you should not feel anything in your throat. It most certainly should not hurt when you sing. Those are indications that something is wrong. You should assess those sensations and talk with your teacher immediately. Sometimes a problem may be very simple to fix, such as by changing your posture. However, you may need your teacher to help you identify and correct other, more difficult problems. The important thing to remember is that pain, in any aspect of your life, should raise a red flag and make you reassess what you were doing when you felt that pain.

### Is Your Voice Tired after You Practice or Perform?

When you sing for 30 minutes, is your voice exhausted? If you sing one song by yourself, do you find that you are hoarse afterward? Fatigue can be an indicator of something wrong with your technique. It may also be simply fatigue. To tell if you should talk to your teacher, you need to see if the tiredness occurs every time you sing that song or if it was a one-time event. If you feel the same fatigue every time you finish a practice session or song, chances are there is an issue with your voice that you need to address. If you have simply had an exhausting day, it may be best to postpone your practicing until you have rested.

### Do You Feel Yourself Improving or Getting Worse over Time?

This is a very big question. If what you are doing is correct, you should sense yourself getting better. You should feel your voice getting stronger. That is how we progress. If, in contrast, you think your abilities have remained the same, or gotten worse, then you need to revisit what you are doing with a teacher.

## CONCLUSION

The foundation of a good, healthy technique separates you from someone who has never had any formal training. This goes for any activity. If this class has given you the desire to continue with your training, then by all means look into private lessons. The one-on-one attention you get during individual lessons will take the technique you have learned here and build on it. If this class will be your only exposure to vocal training, then keep practicing the principles described in this book. Use these principles to hone your skills and improve your singing and speaking abilities. Through proper practice, you will begin to see progress and the fruit of your work.

# CHAPTER 8
# Refining the Song
## Putting Everything Together

In Chapter 2, we talked about the three steps to learning a song. Now that you have spent time learning the proper pitches and rhythms and have merged the words flawlessly into the music, it is time to move to the third and final step of learning a song: putting everything together. This step is, arguably, the most important part of the process. Until now, you have been dealing with each different aspect of the song individually. With this step, you finally begin to think of the song as a whole.

Before we can do that, though, we need to ask one question. Why is this step necessary? If you have learned the notes and the words *correctly,* you are capable of singing the song, right? The answer is both yes and no. Yes, you are able to sing the pitches as presented by the composer. However, you have not dealt with any of the challenges or problems that arise when you sing the piece straight through.

Have you ever played a piece of music on another instrument? Maybe this was a piece of music where the last page, by itself, was fairly simple and straightforward. There may have been a challenging passage or a cadenza that let you really show off, but it was not insurmountable. Then, you went to the beginning of the piece and played it straight through. When you got to the last page, what was once manageable had become the hardest page of music you ever attempted to play. The same thing could occur in almost any sport as well. You are playing a game of football and the pattern you ran a million times during practice becomes very difficult during the game because of the elusiveness of the other team and the length of time you have already been playing. Or you find that the tennis serve you thought you had drilled to perfection suddenly falls apart in an uncoordinated mess when you actually play a set.

That is why *putting it all together* when learning a song is so important. Now you will learn the real nuts-and-bolts about the song. What makes it tick? Where does it get hard? So many students have the misconceived notion that just by looking at the length of a song, they can tell how hard that song is. You will have just as much success determining the quality of a movie by its title alone. Be careful not to fall into this trap. Some one- and two-page songs can be the bane of your existence. Some songs of five pages or more, with just the same thing repeated over and over, are some of the easier songs to sing, though not very interesting. You cannot truly determine the level of difficulty of a piece without looking at it as an integrated whole.

So, what should you ask to make this step in learning a song as productive as possible? First, where are the difficult passages? Is there a high note at the end that you are not used to singing? Does it have some long runs? Maybe it has a note that is in a comfortable part of your range, but you have to hold it for an incredibly long time. Whatever the issue, your first job is to determine what makes this song difficult for you.

Once you have determined the challenges, you are ready to ask the next question. What makes those passages difficult? Have you never sung notes that high or low before? Are you not used to singing in fast tempos? Do you still have problems with breath support that make holding a note for a while nearly impossible? This is where you make the assessment of your own technique with regard to this song. That does not mean that you take all the work you have already put into the song and throw it away because you cannot sing the song. The song was assigned by your teacher because it fit your voice, while still giving you enough of a challenge that you would not be bored. This is simply an assessment of your technique to help you answer the last question: How do I successfully navigate those passages? The way in which you answer this question will establish just how successful you are at singing this song.

Did you know that "cracking" on high notes is rarely the fault of the high note itself? When you crack on a high note, especially a high note that you can usually sing, the true cause of the problem can usually be found in the notes or even pages of music immediately preceding the high note. Often a singer will "throw away" lower notes because they are easy and it does not take any special attention to produce them. However, when the high notes appear, any bad habits that were allowed to creep in because the singer was not thinking about the lower notes suddenly appear when he or she tries to sing a higher note. If you are having problems with a certain note, look at the notes that directly precede the "problem" note. Do you have your mouth open at all? Is your jaw dropped? Is your breath support engaged? If you have answered "no" to any of these questions, *there* is the real culprit robbing you of your high note. If, however, you answered "yes" to all those questions, you may need to move a little more toward the beginning of the song to find out what is wrong. It is also possible that a very small problem has been compounding throughout the song; your teacher can often determine whether this is happening.

Another common issue when putting a song together is the location of breaths throughout the song. This would seem fairly straightforward. As mentioned earlier, if you do not breathe, you have a whole new set of problems apart from how the song sounds. However, where to breathe is always a concern and should be addressed at this point in the process of learning a song. It is almost easier to answer the question, "Where should you *not* breathe?" The quickest answer is in the middle of words. Please, say the full word before taking a breath. That does not mean that you should breathe after every word, either. Unless you are Marilyn Monroe or Anna Nicole Smith singing "Happy Birthday," there is no need to breathe after every word. Use the punctuation in the text to give you clues about where the breaths should be located. Definitely breathe at ending punctuation (e.g., periods, exclamation points). Commas can also provide a good opportunity to take a breath, provided you have enough time in the phrase to do so. When all is said and done, you want to look at what you are saying and how you can say it in the most effective way possible. Speak through the text. If you would not say something a certain way, why would you attempt to sing it that way? Always remember, if you have a question about the appropriateness of a breath within the music, *ask your teacher.*

Let's look back at the original example in this chapter. If the last page of a piece was easy when practiced in isolation, but becomes difficult when put with the rest of the song, you can use another technique to help with this issue. Although we must perform songs from start to finish, nothing says that we cannot put a song together from the end forward to the beginning. Try beginning with the last page. When that page is just the way you want it, add the second-to-last page. Practice both pages together until you perfect them. Repeat this until you are at the beginning of the song. By working backward like this, you become more proactive toward any vocal problems that may arise, rather than being merely reactive. You are addressing issues before they become ingrained in your thinking about the song. Once bad habits become ingrained in the song, you will need to completely relearn the song to eliminate the problems. This is a long, drawn-out process, so avoid it if possible.

## SCORE MAPPING

Score mapping is a technique used by many musicians. Your sheet music becomes a visual learning tool that makes all the information you need available at a glance. This technique assists you with answering the three questions detailed earlier:

1. Where are the difficult passages?
2. What makes them difficult?
3. How do I successfully navigate them?

Whenever you can visually locate these harder passages, you take the first step in overcoming them.

Score mapping involves, at the minimum, a red pencil. It can, however, involve as many different colored pencils as you think are needed. The idea is to make the notation of your song, as a whole, as easy to read as possible. With your pencils at the ready, go through the score, circling and/or otherwise marking any and all items you need to pay special attention to in the music. These may be dynamics, rhythmic articulations, crescendo/decrescendo marks, breath markings (either the composer's or your own), tempo markings, meter changes, and so on. You can choose to do this all with the same color pencil or use many different colors. If you choose many colors, it is important to remain consistent. Mark all your breaths with the same color; mark all your dynamics with the same color; and so on. The idea is to have something that visually calls your attention to a specific issue you must address. If you have breath markings circled in red on the first page and in brown on the next page, it will be more confusing than if you had not marked anything at all.

Score mapping provides the singer another benefit, too: a record that can be memorized along with the text and music. By doing that, you are assured that you will always take a breath at the same place every time you sing the song. You will always put in that same articulation at the same spot, without fail. This is important in helping you get over nervousness and stage fright. Time after time, I see students who knew what they should have done, but because their nerves took over, they forgot everything. By memorizing what you should do just as you do the words in the song, you develop a routine that minimizes uncertainty, which in turn helps minimize any negative effects brought on by nerves. Notice that I did not say "*eliminate* nerves." Score mapping will help keep your nerves from taking over your performance and help you to avoid making simple, silly mistakes.

By seeing all the articulations in the music, you will also become more sensitive to the composer's intent with regard to a song. This, ultimately, helps you in making music and performing a song, a subject addressed in Chapter 9. First, though, we must address the subject of memorization.

## MEMORIZATION

Both teachers and singers debate whether memorizing music is part of the process of learning a song or a different process altogether. It is possible to include memorization in the third step of the learning process, as you are memorizing the song in its entirety. However, for clarity, we are going to deal with memorization separately.

There are many methods that one can use to commit a song to memory. In fact, though there are similarities, there are almost as many ways to memorize as there are teachers of singing. The important thing is for you to choose *one* method and stick with it. The brain capitalizes on repetition and routine to maximize efficiency. If you are constantly jumping from one method of memorization to another, memorizing a song will remain a long, cumbersome process. However, if you stick with one method, your brain will get used to that method and will be able to maximize its memorization efficiency. The result is a streamlined process that you can call upon at will.

Here are a few methods of memorizing songs.

1. *Type:* **Writing Repetition**

   *Description:* The singer writes the text of a song over and over on a piece of paper.

   *Pros:* By utilizing two senses, sight and touch, the text of the song becomes memorized.

   *Cons:* This particular method does not address memorization of the music, only of the text. The singer must make a conscious effort to sing the text while writing, or, at least, go back after the text is memorized and use a different method to memorize the music.

2. *Type:* **Verbal Repetition**

   *Description:* The singer takes a line or phrase of music and sings it repeatedly until the line is committed to memory.

   *Pros:* This method, which is similar to the writing repetition method, allows simultaneous memorization of both text and music.

   *Cons:* Because the song is divided into smaller parts that are easier to memorize, there is a danger that you will lose the continuity of the individual verse or the song as a whole.

   After the song has been memorized, a conscious effort must be made to speak the song and rejuvenate the overall continuity. Because the voice is constantly in action in this method, the singer needs to be careful not to overuse the voice. Furthermore, the singer needs to be aware of the potential of memorizing incorrect or inefficient vocal habits.

3. *Type:* **Cue Cards**

   *Description:* The singer writes the text of each song on cue cards and refers to the cards while attempting to memorize the song.

   *Pros:* The act of writing the text has the same benefits as the writing repetition method, while still allowing the student to sing through the song with the cue cards.

   *Cons:* This method does not afford the benefits of repetition. Additionally, it exchanges one score for another. The singer is merely "weaning" himself or herself from the music. The danger lies in not removing the cue cards in time and constantly needing a visual reference for the music in order to be successful.

4. *Type:* **Cumulative Method**

   *Description:* The singer begins at the beginning of the song, with the music covered (i.e., on a desk or in a lap) and sings through as much of the song as possible from memory. As soon as there is any sort of memory slip, the singer looks at the music and words, reviews the spot where the slip occurred, re-covers the music, and starts singing at the beginning of the song again until another memory slip occurs.

   *Pros:* This method has the singer combining music and words from the beginning. The song, as a whole, is memorized from the start. The process builds on what the singer has already committed to memory. The repetition is used to completely internalize the core of music memorized while expanding the memory toward the final note. Another benefit of this method is that the voice need not be used constantly. This method can be utilized even when a singer is ill and has no voice to sing. Although actual singing does play a part in the process, this method can fill the down time associated with voice loss due to illness.

   *Cons:* This method is a little more laborious than other methods. It requires a larger commitment in both time and patience. The discipline needed to continue to repeat what is already memorized, while adding newer passages, may be a bit much for a student.

These are just a few methods of memorizing songs. This list is not meant to be all-inclusive, nor is it meant to suggest that these are the only ways to memorize. Remember, as mentioned earlier, whatever method you use, stick with it. Use it to memorize a couple of songs. As you work with your chosen method, you will find that memorization becomes faster and more efficient.

# CHAPTER 9
# Performing a Song
## More than Notes on a Page

So that's it! You have learned the basics of your song. You are ready to begin having some real fun. Once you have worked through all the nuts and bolts of your song, you are finally ready to *make some music*. Until now, you have been simply singing the notes and words from the page. Making music is an entirely different process. This is where you get to determine what you do. You make decisions about how to convey what the composer has written. Ultimately, this is where the song becomes yours. This is the exciting, final step in your musical preparation. You will need to have a couple of things in place, in addition to your song, to move through this final step. You will need a sense of adventure, to experiment with different ways of expressing the text until you find what truly conveys your thoughts and ideas. More importantly, you will need an open mind. This will help when you receive constructive criticism from your teacher and peers in your class. They may have certain insights that will help you hone your performance into *exactly* what you want it to be. Are you ready?

## THE PAINTER'S PALETTE AND VOCAL COLORS

Have you ever observed painters while they were painting? Did you see the palette of colors they used? For a single, large piece of canvas, acrylic, or wood, they can certainly get many colors on it! That is not to say that the painter starts with that many colors. Rather, painters need to be masters of blending color. They need to have certain colors to begin with, but by mixing and blending those colors the painters are able to produce the remainder of the colors they will need to finish their paintings. You have heard of the primary colors: red, blue, and yellow. A painter learns that mixing red and blue produces purple; mixing yellow and blue produces green, and so on. With some guidance and some further blending, that same painter can begin to develop different hues within each color. Now it is not a matter of simply green; rather, the painter begins to have access to hunter green, forest green, pea green, light green, and all the rest of the hues in an infinite spectrum. Through this process, using the different hues and tones in each color, the painting is brought to life. The same idea applies to singing a song.

   Each singer begins with the equivalent of the painter's palette: a voice. Singers are also given, from birth, the three primary colors. These colors can be applied to range (high, middle, and low), to the quality of the voice (dark, medium, and bright), and to the dynamics of the voice (loud, medium, and soft). The important thing to remember is that these colors are present. By mixing and blending these colors—applying our own emotional and personal experiences along with the composer's ideas—we can invoke different emotions, attitudes, and styles in each song. Do you see how this could be a lot of fun?

   Now that we have defined vocal colors, or *timbres,* we can talk about how they are used. Different emotions are related to and conveyed by different colors. Some emotions that can be conveyed by a bright sound are happiness, elation, excitement, fear, terror, and anger. A few of the emotions that can be conveyed by a dark sound are sobriety, grief, depression, secrecy, and intimacy. A middle-of-the-road sound can be used like narration of a story: a neutral sound for a neutral idea. There are also ways to add nonmusical sounds, such as screams, laughs, snarls, and growls, to a song if a composer calls for them. Doing so improperly can be detrimental to your overall vocal health and must be done only under the careful supervision of your teacher, to ensure that you are making those sounds in a vocally healthy manner.

## EXPRESSING THE TEXT

The music is what separates a song from poetry. Nevertheless, we still need to refer to the text of each song for clues as to how to express the music. Each composer spent countless hours with the poetry or text in an effort to set it to music in the most effective way possible. It is up to us to use what the composer has given us, incorporate our own experiences, and sing the song the way we feel it should be sung. When we perform a song, audience members should be able to close their eyes and still be able to tell what you are singing about, even if it is in a foreign language. They may not know every word you are singing (unless they are fluent in that language), but they can get the gist of the song from how you are conveying the text.

You can figure out what the composer wants just by listening to the music underneath the vocal line. Does the accompaniment sound "happy" or "sad"? Is it fast or slow? Each of these gives us insight into the thought process of the character in (or of) the song. A song that is fast and "happy" could be a fun-loving, cheerful song, whereas a song that is slow and "sad" might have a depressing subject. But what about a song that is "happy" and slow, or fast and "sad"? Those ideas are not as simple to figure out. That is why we have to look at the text for ourselves.

What subject is the song trying to convey? What has happened to make this song exist? Did you just fall in love? Are you telling a story of the bravery of soldiers who were captured and eventually died? Now is the time to determine the overall concept that you and the composer are trying to convey. You could even do some research to discover what was happening during the composer's life when this piece was written. From a background of such information, we can look at specific passages that are included in the song.

Scrutinize each individual line of text for what it is trying to communicate. Where is the natural rise and fall of the line? (This can be determined by speaking through the text and determining how you would speak each line.) We do not talk on one level. As we speak, the voice rises and falls with the inflection of each word. There is an almost musical direction in how we naturally speak. By speaking through the text, you will notice that the musical line is probably close to the natural rise and fall of the spoken text. *The composer has done much of the work for you.* There is no need to reinvent the wheel. Your job is to enhance what the composer has given you.

One thing that may help you at this point is to record how you speak through the text. As you listen to the recording, pay specific attention to the direction of each line. Take note of how you read through each phrase. Where are the important words? Where did you breathe? Did you breathe because you were running out of air, or was there some dramatic purpose for the breath? From there, take your notes on the recording and relate them to how you sing the song. Is it possible to take the breaths in the same place as when you spoke the text? Does the music agree with you about which words are important and which words are secondary? Make the necessary adjustments to your notes, and you are off and running in this process of making music. On a side note, the score mapping that we talked about in Chapter 8 can make this step easier by providing visual emphasis for aspects of the music that require special attention.

## THE EYES AND FACE: THE TRUE GATEWAY TO OUR SOULS

Did you know that you can hear a smile? Try it. Have friends close their eyes and listen to you speak a line or two of text. At certain times while you are reading out loud, smile. Ask your friends to raise their hands when they think you are smiling. You will be surprised at how often they can *hear* you smiling. It is important for you to realize this, so you do not neglect the importance of facial expressions when singing. Every time you speak, you use your face. Your mouth may smile or frown. Your eyes may squint or open wide. Your eyebrows may move up and down with the emphasis of certain words. Be aware that this is happening every day (see Figure 9.1).

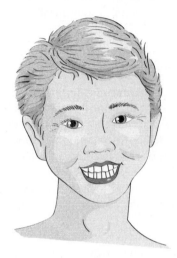 

Happy? Content?                                     Angry? Sad?

**Figure 9.1** Facial expressions

Try it in front of a mirror. Stand in front of the mirror and pretend that you are talking to your significant other. First, try talking to this person about something really exciting that happened to you. Take note of what happens facially as you go through your story. Then, pretend to have a fight with that person. Really yell at him or her! Let that person know that you are angry. Do you see everything that has changed? Once you are aware of how your face works when you let your true emotions show, you can begin to incorporate those same expressions into your songs, at will. It does take practice, though.

As with any practice, you need to be in front of a mirror. Sing through the first line of text. Is that how you want to express that line? Experiment; have fun. Even though you may be sad and singing about breaking up with the love of your life, try singing that song with a giddy smile on your face. If you are singing about how wonderful your life is, try looking as if someone had just run over the pet that you have had since you were a baby. Of course, this does not mean that you will perform the song this way, but after this exercise you will know how *not* to express the text, which can be just as beneficial as figuring out how you *are* going to express the text. Additionally, you may find that singing with your eyes sad, but a slight smile on your face, adds a different facet or aspect to your performance. All of a sudden you see sadness but with a look of relief. Always remember the painter's palette. You have just added another color to it. Congratulations!

## Gestures

The debate over the quantity of gestures, to be used through the course of one song, can get pretty heated. Some believe that your hands should be completely still while you sing. A lot of hand movement can be distracting. Others believe that when the spirit moves you to wave your hands, you should wave your hands. Both ideas are equally good and have their place in learning to make music. If you do not move your hands at all, you may come across as stiff and rigid. This can cause tension, which then leads to vocal issues. If you are the type of person who talks with your hands, locking your hands in place is only asking for problems. However, if you are constantly flailing about when you sing a song, it can get quite distracting. If you are not a person who talks with your hands, being asked to use gestures throughout your performance may only add tension to your body—then you are, again, back at square one.

It seems that a good rule of thumb for gestures is: *less is more*. You want to be free to move your hands when appropriate, but you do not want people to think that your hand has a mind of its own. A good gesture has three characteristics:

1. It has been practiced over and over until it is as natural a movement as it can possibly be.
2. It accents a point in the music you are trying to emphasize.
3. It fits with both the mood and the style of the music.

Let's look at these individually. First, as with everything else in this book, you *must* practice your gestures. This has to be done in front of a mirror or a friend who will give you honest feedback. This is the only way to determine if what you are doing is effective and conveys exactly what you are trying to say. More often than not, you will find that the gesture should be bigger than what you are doing. You may think that you have brought your hand up to your waist when in reality it has only moved an inch. One gesture can be seen by everyone watching; the other looks more like a nervous twitch. Unless you see it for yourself, or have someone else see it and comment, you will always think you are doing enough.

Second, a well-placed gesture enhances the idea and really expresses the current mood of the singer. If you bring your hand to your heart and then quickly swat it away, that is a powerful gesture. If you are singing about the love you thought you had, but the other person was cheating, the gesture becomes a visual exclamation point to the phrase. The audience sympathizes with your problem. However, if you do that same gesture and you are talking about how your heart is filled with joy and your life is complete, one gesture becomes two in the eyes of the audience. The first gesture is of you bringing your hand to your heart, obviously feeling so wonderful and full of life. The second gesture becomes you swatting the invisible bee that was threatening to sting you while you sang. You can see how that would be more than a little distracting. You need to use gestures at well-chosen points of emphasis only.

The third factor is a bit less obvious and a bit more intellectual. The gesture has to fit with the style and mood of the music. This applies to facial expressions as well. If you are downtrodden and depressed, you definitely do not want to be smiling from ear to ear (unless you are trying to convey "psychotic"). Also, if you are singing an old English folk song ending with the word "peace," you probably do not want the final gesture to be a big peace sign over your head. Both gestures have their place, but not necessarily in the same song. During this step, you remove yourself somewhat from the character of the piece. Gestures used in today's vernacular may not necessarily be appropriate to songs from the last couple of centuries. Your teacher can help you with stylistic ideas of a given time period.

Now you have all the tools necessary to successfully perform a song. You have learned the notes and the words, and you have put everything together. You took a song and made it your own by expressing the text, adding facial expressions, and determining what kinds of gestures, if any, you wanted to use. All that is left is to stand up in front of someone or a group of people and demonstrate what you can do. You have worked hard; now you reap the rewards for your efforts.

# CHAPTER 10
# Living with Your Voice
## Vocal Do's and Don'ts

You have now learned many of the fundamental aspects of singing. You have learned how to practice, how to learn and memorize a song, and how to perform a song. There is one aspect of singing left to be discussed: the care of your instrument. You may assume that you know how to take care of your own voice; after all, the voice is an internal instrument and you have been using it since birth, right?. That could not be further from the truth. If anything, the exact opposite is true. We know how to *abuse* our voices. We do it every day. Whether it is screaming for the home team at a sporting event, drinking alcohol, or talking while we have laryngitis, we have all been guilty of abusing our voices at one time or another. The problem is that we sometimes do not know what is or is not abusive or harmful to the voice.

## VOCAL DON'TS

The only way to combat vocal misuse and abuse is to identify the causes and correct the behavior. Many things can injure your vocal cords. Some of the problems can cause immediate damage, such as hoarseness and vocal hemorrhage, whereas others cause damage over a longer period of time, such as vocal nodules and polyps (essentially blisters on the vocal folds). The important thing to remember is that damage is damage. It should be treated and reversed as soon as possible.

One of the most common sources of vocal misuse is *overuse,* talking and/or singing after your voice has clearly become fatigued. This can be caused by individual things, like talking for a long time during a car ride, or by a combination of events, like practicing *and* participating in class *and* talking on the phone nonstop. You finish your activities and your voice feels tired. The muscles in your throat may or may not be exhausted. Even more, you just do not feel like using your voice anymore. Then your friends come over to visit. Away you go, talking up a storm and using your voice after it has already signaled its fatigue. That is when problems can occur.

When you first begin to feel any type of fatigue in your throat, you need to stop immediately and assess the cause. If it is something that can be fixed or adjusted right then, do it. A good example of this is adjusting your posture from a hunched-over position to a more upright and straight stance that facilitates easier breath support. If the conditions cannot be adjusted, stop the activity and rest your voice. Once you go beyond that point to fatigue, you risk serious injury. As a point of reference, here is a list of common vocal misuses:

- overuse (includes overpracticing)
- yelling
- screaming
- laughing violently (cackling, chortling, guffawing, etc.)
- coughing (especially dry coughs)
- clearing the throat

- whispering
- not warming up the voice before use

How many of these things have you done before? Now that you know these activities can injure your voice, you can take steps to avoid doing them. However, the behaviors mentioned in the list are not the only things that can injure your voice. Certain substances we consume can have an adverse effect on our voices. Figure 10.1 is a chart of various popular consumables and their adverse effects on the voice.

| Consumable | Effect |
|---|---|
| Smoking | Dries out and thickens the vocal folds. Also creates more coughing. |
| Alcohol | Produces a numbing effect throughout your body. You do not know if you are doing damage to your voice or not. |
| Caffeine | Drying effect on the vocal folds. |
| Antihistamines (allergy medicines) | Used to "dry" up excess drainage from nasal passages, but also dries out vocal folds. |

**Figure 10.1** Popular consumables and their effects on the voice

As you can see, our voices are affected by many things. However, that does not mean that they are fragile. Amazingly, our voices are capable of handling the abuse we give them and coming back for more. However, as you get older, the voice stops being as resilient. Unfortunately, by that time, bad habits are so ingrained that they may be impossible to reverse. That is why it is important to make positive changes now.

## VOCAL DO'S

What is a person to do? With all of the things that can adversely affect the voice, is there anything that has a positive effect? Certainly. There are many things you can do that will be beneficial to your voice. Addressing the behaviors mentioned in the preceding section is a great first step. The first three misuses listed—overuse, yelling, and screaming—are not ever necessary. If you want to cheer at a sporting event or concert, find other, nonverbal means of doing it, or, at the very least, use a souvenir megaphone. That will amplify your voice without your having to scream. Also, remember to use proper breath support *at all times*. This is extremely important. This one thing alone can greatly reduce the wear and tear on your voice.

The next three misuses on the list should be addressed for their causes. What is causing you to cough or clear your throat? Do you have a cold or respiratory infection? If so, addressing that should eliminate your need to cough. A number of things can cause your need to clear your throat: acid reflux, lactose intolerance and asthma, to name but a few. Getting these under control should help you minimize or eliminate that behavior as well. As for whispering, there are times when whispering is unavoidable; however, keep it to a minimum. When we whisper, our throat muscles tend to tighten, especially if we are whispering and do not think we are being heard. As the "whispering" gets louder and louder, the throat gets more and more tense. That quickly causes vocal fatigue. When in doubt, write it down and pass a note.

The last misuse is something we dealt with in Chapter 3. You should always warm up your voice. Whether it is vocalizing before you sing a song, or sighing in the shower first thing in the morning before you talk, warming up the voice is essential to maintaining vocal health throughout the course of your life.

There are other things you can do that have a positive effect on your voice. The following lists a few suggestions:

- *Sleep.* Make sure you get plenty of rest. The body, including your voice, needs time to rejuvenate.

- *Drink plenty of water.* Water keeps your body hydrated and everything in your body lubricated. When you stay hydrated, the vocal folds stay lubricated and ready for action. Also, if you need to take medicine for allergies, drink plenty of water to counteract the drying effects of the antihistamines.

- *Gargle with warm salt water.* If you work out your legs until they are exhausted, what is a great way to help them feel better? A warm soak in a bathtub or spa. Think of gargling with warm salt water like that soak after a workout. It soothes and relaxes your throat. It may not taste great, but it is effective. Please do not swallow!

- *Exercise.* We all recognize the benefits of exercise for the rest of the body and overall health, but did you know that it helps with singing, too? Exercise helps you develop better muscle tone and abdominal strength. This, combined with increased oxygen to your body tissues, aids in increasing your breath support and the efficiency of your breath support.

- *Vocal rest.* Yes, rest has already been mentioned; however, this is quite important. Even if you do not have the luxury of resting your body, you may still be able to rest your voice. Try resting your voice when you are driving or riding as a passenger in a car. There are no cars made today that allow the driver to sit at the optimum angle for correct breath support. That means that every time you talk, you are using your throat and throat muscles rather than your breath support. Have you ever gone on an extended car trip only to have your voice be quite tired when you arrived at your destination? That is the reason.

Those are just some suggestions for overall vocal health. Your teacher will have many more. If you feel that something you are doing may be negatively affecting your voice, do not be afraid to let your teacher know. Your teacher can work with you to help correct that issue and get you back on the road to successful singing. Remember, we each are given only one voice. What we choose to do with it is up to us.

# Introduction to the Song Anthology

Now it is time to put the theory of singing into practice. The following song anthology is designed to give you a cross-section of music from various genres (sacred, popular, stage, classical, etc.). I chose the following songs based on the pieces and styles of music that have been selected or requested in my voice classes over the past few years. Although I was not able to include every song that has been requested, I did try to include the most popular ones. When a certain requested song was especially difficult, I substituted another song of the same type.

The difficulty levels of the songs cover the spectrum from easier hymns to challenging opera arias. This provides a broad range of music that reflects the wide range of musical ability of the students registering for voice classes today. It would not be useful or even possible to have a song anthology that did not include a broad range of styles. Some students may be coming into the class after having been in their state's all-state choir all four years of high school. Even though they have not chosen music as a field of study, those students require more challenging literature. Other students may have never even thought about singing except for with the radio. For them, easier songs have been included. It is impossible to predict every situation, but this anthology can do a good job of meeting most needs.

I have also included a section of duets for use in class. In some instances, a student may have a terrific voice but not be comfortable singing alone. These duets attempt to provide music for such students to sing with another person, to help relieve any solo anxiety. These duets are not easy, but they can be fun and engaging for the proper voices.

When working with these songs, it is important to remember that the singers will, more than likely, not sound like the artists who made some of these songs popular. In fact, it can be detrimental to the voice even to attempt to sound like someone else. Each student should strive to make the song his or her own, and all students should use the voice they have with the technique they are learning.

Included with each song are brief notes about how to perform or what to watch out for in that song. These notes are called "*The scoop.*" Because it is impossible, in such a small space, to cover all the aspects of each song, "*The scoop*" highlights some basic information for the student about possible trouble spots or overall issues to be addressed. These notes can help both in selecting a song and for learning and performing the song.

Care has been taken to make the accompaniment CDs as beneficial as possible for the learning of each song. When the melody line is not played as part of the actual piano accompaniment, an additional melody line has been added to a separate track to assist in learning. We have also included a pronunciation track for the foreign-language songs. Finally, an additional step has been taken for the duet recordings. In the track that contains the melody and accompaniment, each part can be isolated by adjusting the speaker balance to the right or left speaker. This will make it much easier for the student to hear the individual part while learning the song.

# The Songs

**SACRED MUSIC**

## *Amazing Grace* (traditional)

**The scoop:**   This is one of the most famous hymns around. Like most hymns, it is easy to just sing the notes and words. However, because every note repeats for each verse, the repetition can lead to an unenthusiastic performance. Think about what you are singing and try to convey the text. That will help you keep the song energized.

### Amazing Grace

Romans 5:15
John Newton, *pub.* 1779; *v.4* Unknown, *pub.*1829

New Britain
Unknown, *pub.*1829

1. A - maz - ing grace! How sweet the sound That saved a wretch like me!
2. 'Twas grace that taught my heart to fear, And grace my fears re - lieved;
3. Through man - y dan - gers, toils and snares, I have al - read - y come;
4. When we've been there ten thou - sand years, Bright shin - ing as the sun,

I once was lost, but now am found; Was blind, but now I see.
How pre - cious did that grace ap - pear The hour I first be - lieved.
'Tis grace hath brought me safe thus far, And grace will lead me home.
We've no less days to sing God's praise Than when we'd first be - gun.

John Newton, pub. 1779

### *Angels Through the Night* (arr. Philip Kern)

**The scoop:**   This wonderful arrangement combines two popular songs into one: "All Through the Night" and "Angels Watching over Me." Be careful of the second verse. The melody is slightly different from the initial statement. The tendency is to sing it the other way, but that is not what is written. Also, starting at the last "Soft the drowsy hours," you begin the climax of the piece. Make sure your support is fully engaged and do not oversing. The piano has an ascending line that provides a wonderful increase in intensity, but it can make the singer give too much vocally.

Angels Through The Night
(All Through the Night/All Night, All Day)

peace at - tend thee, All through the night.

*cresc.*

Soft the drow - sy hours are creep - ing, Hill and vale in

slum - ber sleep - ing, God, His lov - ing vig - il keep - ing,

## *Ave Maria* (Schubert)

**The scoop:** This beautiful piece was originally written in German with different words. (The original words were from "The Lady of the Lake" by Sir Walter Scott.) The Latin words presented here are the more traditional and famous words to the song. They are taken from the Catholic prayer "Hail Mary." This piece is deceptively difficult. It requires a good foundation in breath support to successfully navigate the long melodic lines found throughout the piece.

### Ave Maria
High Voice

Franz Schubert Op.52. No 6.

Edition Peters.

# Ave Maria
## Low Voice

Franz Schubert, Op. 52, No. 6

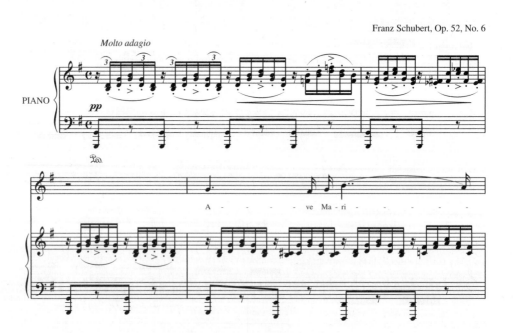

### *I Walked Today Where Jesus Walked* (O'Hara)

**The scoop:** This terrific song by Geoffrey O'Hara is appropriate during most of the church year; however, it can be especially effective when sung during Lent. Watch out for the key change and accompaniment change that occur at "My pathway led through Bethlehem." The piano moves from an eighth-note accompaniment to a sixteenth-note accompaniment. The tendency is to rush when singing. The beat stays the same; the piano is the only thing that changes. At "I picked my heavy burden up," the accompaniment changes to a chordal repetition. This is in preparation for the tone painting that occurs at "I climbed the hill of Calvary." Stay relaxed through the end of the piece. If you let your emotions dictate how you sing this, you will start to get tense as the climax of the piece moves higher and higher. If that happens, the phrase "Where on the Cross He died!" will not be as secure and meaningful as it can be.

## I Walked Today Where Jesus Walked

Daniel S. Twohig

Geoffrey O'Hara

climbed the Hill of Cal-va-ry, I climbed the Hill of

Cal-va-ry,____ Where on the Cross He died!____ I

walked to-day where Je-sus walked And felt Him close to me!

### *The Lord Is My Shepherd* (Kaplan)

**The scoop:** In this wonderful setting of Psalm 23, the composer has set a musical line to begin higher in the voice and move down. This gives the singer an opportunity to keep the voice feeling high in the head right from the start, without trying to overpower the sound by using a lot of chest resonance. Be aware, when attempting the high G on the word "over," that a softer "r" will help keep the voice from constricting on the higher note. The word could be thought of as "ovuh," if necessary.

# The Lord is My Shepherd

Music by
Abraham Kaplan

*Melody line may be omitted from the piano part.

good ____ ness and mer-cy - shall fol-low me all the days of my life: ____ and I will dwell in the house of the Lord ____ for ev - er. ____ The Lord is my shep-herd; I shall not want, ___ I shall not want, ___ I shall not want. ____

## *Oy Hanukkah, Oy Hanukkah* (traditional)

**The scoop:**   In this traditional Hanukkah song, the words are slightly different from what you may be used to singing. Take care to let the new words be heard in their full value. Also, it is best to learn this song at a slower tempo and work up to the brisker tempo that is presented here. Proper technique should always be observed, practiced, and solidly in place *before* you attempt to speed things up. Since this is a faster song, it is played through twice on the accompaniment recording.

## *The Old Rugged Cross* (traditional)

**The scoop:**   This is another popular hymn. Unlike "Amazing Grace," this one has a verse and refrain. The difficult part of this hymn occurs during the refrain, when the melody moves toward the upper middle part of the voice. Take care to approach those notes with proper breath support and no tension in the throat. If your throat is constricted, the refrain will be extremely difficult to sing.

The Old Rugged Cross

Galatians 6:14
G. B., 1913

George Bennard, 1913

## *Star Of The East* (Kennedy)

**The scoop:**   This charming Christmas/Advent song remains, for the most part, in the comfortable part of the vocal range for lower voices. There is an optional duet at the end of the piece, but it is not required; it is just as nice as a solo. The thing to be careful of is the chords in the piano that support the voice. Make sure that the musical line continues to flow and does not get choppy or broken up when you are singing.

Star Of The East

(Melody, Star Of The Sea)

Music by Amanda Kennedy
Words by George Cooper

Fear-less and tran-quil, we look up to thee! Know-ing thou beam'st thro' e -
Smiles of a Sav-iour are mir-ror'd in thee! Glimps-es of Heav'n in thy

- ter - ni - ty! Help us to fol-low where thou still dost guide,
-light_ we see! Guide us still on-ward to that bles-sed shore,

Pil - grims of earth so wide._____ Star Of The East, thou
Af - ter earth's toil is o'er!_____

o'er us still till life hath ceased, Beam on, bright star, sweet Beth-le-hem star!

## When I Survey the Wondrous Cross (traditional)

**The scoop:**  This is a terrific song for a new student with a very limited vocal range. It is a powerful hymn that does not go too high or too low. The important thing to focus on is the words. The text will guide the musical direction of each phrase.

### When I Survey the Wondrous Cross

Galatians 6:14                                                                                      Hamburg
Isaac Watts, *pub*.1707                                                          Lowell Mason, 1824

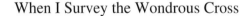

1. When I sur - vey the won-drous cross On which the Prince of glo - ry died,
2. For - bid it, Lord, that I should boast, Save in the death of Christ my God!
3. Were the whole realm of na - ture mine, That were a pres - ent far too small;

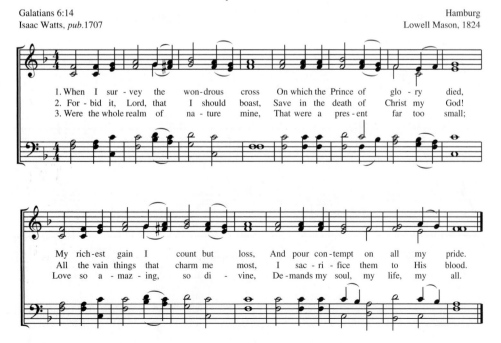

My rich-est gain I count but loss, And pour con-tempt on all my pride.
All the vain things that charm me most, I sac - ri - fice them to His blood.
Love so a - maz - ing, so di - vine, De - mands my soul, my life, my all.

## OLDIES BUT GOODIES

### *Beautiful Dreamer* (Foster)

**The scoop:**    This popular song by Stephen Foster is fairly straightforward. The difficult part about this song is the 9/8 meter. For a beginning student, this may seem too daunting. Try to feel this song as if it were in 3 with triplets for each beat. This will help ease any anxiety over thinking about nine beats to a measure, and will also ensure a smoother melodic line.

Beautiful Dreamer
SERENADE

Words and Music by
Stephen C. Foster

stream let and sea;_____ Then will all clouds of sor - row de - part,_____

Beau - ti - ful dream - er, a - wake un - to me!_____

Beau - ti - ful dream - er, a - wake un - to me!_____

Ad Lib.

A Tempo.

*Clayian.*

Published by W.M.A. Pond & Co.

### *Because* (d'Hardelot)

**The scoop:**    This song, long a pillar of the wedding service repertoire, is included for the more adventurous singer. The inclusion of the optional notes does make the song more accessible to novice singers, but care should be taken when selecting this for performance. The range stays a bit higher in the voice than other songs. The way the notes are approached also adds to the difficulty. The stepwise movement to the high notes adds to the thrill of the music, but make sure that your breath support is constantly engaged and that air is fueling the sound as the notes ascend. There can be no "grabbing" the sound by closing the throat.

## Because

Music by Guy D'hardelot
Words by Ward Teschemacher

love, _____ And hold my hand and lift mine eyes a - bove, ___ A

wi - - der world of hope and joy I see, _____ Be -

- cause _____ you come to me.

Be - cause you speak to me in accents

## *Dixie* (Emmett)

**The scoop:** In this famous minstrel tune, you will find a welcome blend between ease of range and thrilling higher notes. The song itself does not venture that high. It stays, predominantly, in the lower to middle part of the range. However, it does have the occasional high note on the words "away" and "south." When these notes are sung, avoid the natural diphthong (two vowel sounds together) for as long as possible. You will have more success by singing on the first vowel sound and adding the diphthong at the very end.

### Dixie

Dan D. Emmett
Edited and Arranged by Granville Bantock

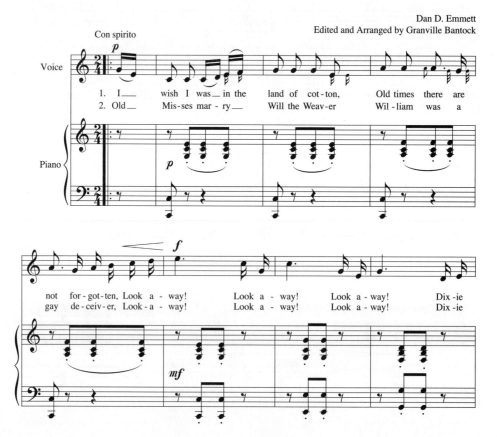

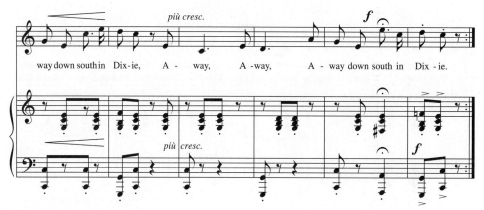

### *Dreamy Hawaii* (Vandersloot)

**The scoop:** This fun song reflects the spirit of the Hawaiian islands. Throughout each verse, the piano mimics the sound of a ukulele. Strive for a smooth legato line over the unique accompaniment. The last two verses of the song can be sung as a duet, but it is not necessary to do so. The notes have been included so as to leave the decision to the singer(s). Note that the first three verses deal with Hawaii almost as a secondary idea; the love left behind is at the forefront of the singer's mind. Then, for the final verse, the focus turns fully to the islands themselves, with an interesting tempo marking *Con amore,* which means "with love."

## Dreamy Hawaii

Music by F. W. Vandersloot
Lyric by Ray Sherwood

Sly lit-tle stars are wink - ing, Sweet summer breez - es sigh; _____

Dream-ing of my Ha - wai - i, Stroll-ing 'neath skies of blue; _____

Chas-ing Ha - wai - ian rain - bows, Build-ing love cas-tles with you. _____ There is

Poco animato

some - one sweet and ten - der, Like a flow - er in its splen - dor, That is

*mf*

With my gui - tar a - ring - ing, - Mel - o - dies soft and low; _____

Just like the i - vy cling - ing, Love holds us with its charms, _____

Dream - ing of sweet Ha - wai - i, Finds me in some bod - y's arms. _____

Con amore

Per - fume scent - ed breez - es All re - turn a - new, _____

*mp*

The sheet music lyrics:
Fair-y -land of ro - mance, In my dreams of you;____ ,

Stray-ing thro' the wild - wood, Hap - py days of yore,____

Dreams of my Ha -wai - i; Bring back once more.____

### *Jeanie with the Light Brown Hair* (Foster)

**The scoop:** In this wonderfully lyric song by Stephen Foster, the singer is asked to reflect on the image of this "goddess" among women. The song is meant to be sung with a somewhat subdued tone, but remember not to forsake the beauty and energy of proper singing in order to sing this song softly. Learn how to sing this song using a healthy technique before ever attempting to tone down the sound for musical effect.

# Jeanie With The Light Brown Hair

Poetry & Music by
Stephen C. Foster

Hap - py as the dai - sies that dance on her way,

Ma - ny were the wild notes her mer - ry voice would pour.

Ma - ny were the blithe birds that war - bled them: o'er Oh!_____ I

dream of Jea - nie with the light brown hair,

Float - ing, like a va - por, on the soft sum - mer air.

*Ital - - - len - - - tan - - - dn.*

*8va*

*tempo.*

I long for Jea - nie with the gay dawn smile,

Ra - diant in glad - ness warm with win - ning guile; I

long          for  Jea - nie,  and  my    heart    bows     low,

Ne - ver  more    to  find  her  where    the    bright    wa - ters  flow.

*Ral - - - - len - - - tan - - - do.*

*8va*

*tempo.*

Copyright 1882 by Mrs. Mathew D. Wiley and Mrs. Maria Foster Welsh.

## The John Brown Song (traditional)

**The scoop:**  This song is one of the first versions of what eventually became "The Battle Hymn of the Republic." Students will recognize the tune as soon as they hear it. However, the words are much different from the "Battle Hymn." This means that the melody is different as well. The notes are the same, but rhythms may or may not be what you are used to singing. Take care to learn this song properly the first time. If you do not, it will be twice as hard to fix any problems once you have learned the wrong notes.

# The John Brown Song

### *Leave Me with a Smile* (Koehler & Burtnett)

**The scoop:** This charming song uses a large number of accidentals (altered notes) throughout. This gives the song the sound of the Roaring Twenties, but it can become a fairly significant issue for the beginning singer. If singers are aware of this before they start to learn the music, many of those altered notes will not be a problem. Remember that the melody is played in the accompaniment. By listening to the piano and being sensitive to what is played, you will be able to have some fun with this song.

## Leave Me With A Smile

By Chas. Koehler
and Earl Burtnett

days that used to be;    I a-wait the sun-set,    for now you're leav-ing me.

Chorus

Tho'_____ it's    time for - part-ing,    and_____ my    tears are start-ing,

Leave    me    with    a    smile _____    Tho'_____ your

heart    may    cry,    dear;    When_____ you    say    good - bye,    dear,    Leave    me

### *M-O-T-H-E-R* (Morse)

**The scoop:**   When performing this song, it is important to maintain the two distinct contrasts that are written into this piece. The first contrast is between the verse and the chorus. The verse tells the story and is focused on the singer. The chorus is all about that most special word, which the singer not only knows but can spell: *mother*. The second contrast happens within the chorus. Emphasize each of the letters as they are spelled. The danger is in running them together with the rest of the phrase. By placing a little more emphasis on the individual letters as they appear, you will find it much easier to convey the idea of spelling the word.

## M-O-T-H-E-R
### A Word That Means The World To Me

Melody by Theodore Morse
Lyric by Howard Johnson

I've been a-round the world, you bet, But nev-er went to school, Hard
When I was but a ba-by, long be-fore I learned to walk, While

knocks are all I seem to get, Per-haps I've been a fool; But
ly-ing in my cra-dle, I would try my best to talk; It

still, some ed - u - ca - ted folks, sup - posed to be so swell, Would
was - n't long, be - fore I spoke, and all the neigh - bors heard, My

fail, if they were called up - on a sim - ple word to spell. Now
folks were ve - ry proud of me for "Moth - er" was the word. Al -

if you'd like to put me to a test, _____ There's
though I'll nev - er lay a claim to fame, _____ I'm

one dear name that I can spell the best: _____
sat - is - fied that I can spell this name: _____

### *Over There* (Cohan)

**The scoop:**    In this spirited and very famous song by George M. Cohan, the singer is asked to change the musical line throughout the verses. Each verse begins with two moving eighth-note lines as the singer sings, "Johnny get your gun," followed by two smooth quarter-note lines. It was this transition between moods that masterfully captured the soldier's thoughts during World War I: the thrill and patriotism of fighting for the United States and the moment of pause at the thought of leaving home. Then, during the chorus, the vocal line takes on a bugle-like quality that further drives home the "call to arms" idea and the march off to war.

## Over There

By George M. Cohan

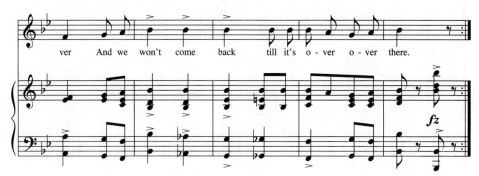

### *Smilin' Through* (Penn)

**The scoop:**    The meaning of this song is left to each singer to determine on his or her own. However, the music brings to mind a wonderful memory and reflection on times past. Try to find something within the context of the emotion of the song to help convey the text. Musically, the vocal line soars to its highest point when the text talks about the little green gate and all the long years, as if those two aspects of the memory create the highest anticipation and most elation in the mind of the singer. Then, at the end of the verse, there is an abruptness in the musical line as the singer takes a moment to recall the experience before expressing it. The sensitive singer will have a wonderful time performing this song.

## Smilin' Through

Lyric and Music by
Arthur A. Penn

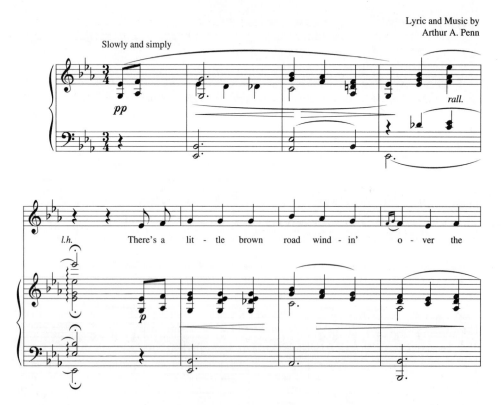

hill To a lit - tle white cot by the sea;_____ There's a

little green gate At whose trel - lis I wait, While two

eyes o' blue Come smil - in' through At me!_____ There's a

gray lock or two in the brown of the hair, There's some

sil - ver in mine, too, I see;_____ But in

all the long years When the clouds brought their tears, Those two

eyes o' blue Kept smil - in' through At me!_____

MCMXIX by M. Witmark & Sons.

## *Tenting on the Old Camp Ground* (Kittredge)

**The scoop:** In this somber war song, soldiers are reminiscing about home and the end of the fighting. The song itself does not venture to any extremes of range, so it is important to focus on what is being said and how to convey the words. That is what will make this song special. Otherwise, it is just another two-verse song. One thing to be aware of is the syncopation at the end of the chorus, on "Tenting tonight." This is reflected in the piano, but it is possible to overlook that rhythm the first time through.

# Tenting on the Old Camp Ground

Words and Music by Walter Kittredge
Edited and Arranged by Granville Bantock

1. We're ___ tent - ing to-night on the old Camp - ground,
2. We've been tent - ing to-night on the old Camp - ground,

Give us a song to cheer Our ___ wear - y hearts, a
Think-ing of days gone by, Of the loved ones at home that

song of home, And friends ___ we love so dear.
gave us the hand, And the tear that said "Good - bye!"

*Chorus*

Ma - ny are the hearts that are wear - y to-night, Wish-ing for the war to

### The Yankee Doodle Boy (Cohan)

**The scoop:** This famous, patriotic song incorporates the original tune "Yankee Doodle" into its musical fabric. There is even a snippet of the "Star-Spangled Banner" thrown in for good measure. All of this combines to make it a fun piece to perform. The range goes a bit higher than other songs in this anthology, with a written F on top. Although it does not stay up there for long, you need to be aware of it and prepare accordingly. Also, though the refrain of the song sits a little higher than some other songs, the musical lines start high and descend, which is certainly easier for beginning singers than starting low and moving high.

# The Yankee Doodle Boy

George M. Cohan

CHORUS.

I'm a Yan-kee Doo-dle Dan - - - dy, A
Yan - kee Doo-dle, do or die;_____ A
real live nep-hew of my Un - cle Sam's,
Born on the Fourth of Ju - ly._____ I've

### *You're a Grand Old Flag* (Cohan)

**The scoop:**   This song is great fun to sing. In George M. Cohan's classic patriotic tune, you will also find a small fragment of "Dixie" incorporated into the verse. This song really gets the listener's toes tapping, literally. However, be cautious of that excitement. The danger in this song lies in getting too wrapped up in the emotions and excitement of the music and forgetting about the fundamentals of singing. This song does venture higher in the range, so make sure you are singing all of the notes correctly. When that is assured, then you can have some real fun performing this song.

### You're A Grand Old Flag

George M. Cohan

list - ning to the mu - sic of a mil - i - ta - ry band, An - y

tune like "Yan - kee Doo - dle" simp - ly sets me off my noo - dle, It's that

pa - tri - ot - ic some - thing that no one can un - der - stand.

"Way down South in the land of cot - ton," mel - - o - dy un -

## POPULAR MUSIC

### *Have You Ever Really Loved a Woman* (Kamen; as sung by Bryan Adams)

**The scoop:**   This song is from the movie *Don Juan DeMarco*. The song has a Spanish feel to it that reflects the story of the movie. A second line of notes is included that can make this song a duet; be aware that both parts approach the upper end of the tonal range. If done by a man or men, it is wise to approach those upper notes using falsetto. It is important to sing those notes as healthily as possible.

### Have You Ever Really Loved A Woman?

Music by
Michael Kamen
Lyrics by
Bryan Adams and Robert John "Mutt" Lange

### *How Do I Live* (Warren; as sung by Trisha Yearwood)

**The scoop:** Here is another song made famous by a movie; this time the movie was *Con Air*. The range of this song is not nearly as wide as the first song in this section. The important thing to watch out for is the ascending line "How do I ever, ever get by." Resist the tendency to oversing on the top note; if you oversing it, it will sound out of place. Remember to approach the note with proper support and finesse.

## How Do I Live

### *Minnie, the Moocher* (Calloway and Mills; as sung by Cab Calloway)

**The scoop:** This popular tune was one of Mr. Calloway's signature pieces. It requires an ease of tempo and a sense of fun during the "heidi-ho" section. Allow the spirit of the music to loosen the rhythmic values of some of the notes. This will help to properly convey the music. Additionally, it is common for the various scat sections to be taken as fast as possible, in an attempt to show off what Cab Calloway was best known for doing. However, it is important to learn the rhythms, *as written,* first. If you do not learn the proper notes and rhythms *before* loosening up certain rhythmic values, you run the risk of making the rhythms sound like a mistake rather than extra inflections of certain words.

## Minnie, The Moocher

Words and Music by
Cab Calloway and Irving Mills

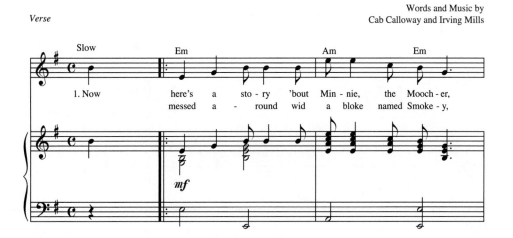

dee   de   dee)   Ho   de   ho___   de   ho_   (Ho   de   ho - o   de ho)
dah   do   dah)   Ho   de                                                2. She

Ho___   de ho_____   Poor   Min,  Poor  Min,  Poor   Min.

### *My Heart Will Go On* (Horner; as sung by Celine Dion)

**The scoop:**   This famous song from the movie *Titanic* was made popular by Celine Dion. The long, sweeping lines in this piece require a firm grasp of the concept of breath support. The music does not venture to the extremes of the range, even after the infamous key change toward the end. Nevertheless, the dangerous thing about this song is trying to sound exactly like Celine Dion. In attempting to mimic Celine Dion, you may manipulate your voice in a negative way and create tension or other vocal problems. This version is not identical to Dion's interpretation; that is precisely why it is *her* interpretation. Strive to find your own voice within the context of this popular song.

# My Heart Will Go On
## (Love Theme from "Titanic")

Music by
James Horner
Lyrics by
Will Jennings

### *R-E-S-P-E-C-T* (Redding; as sung by Aretha Franklin)

**The scoop:**   In this fun song, follow some of the same ideas described in "the scoop" for "Minnie, the Moocher." An ease of tempo and loosening of certain rhythmic values will help to convey the text properly. However, it is important to learn the rhythms as written first. If you do not learn the proper notes and rhythms *before* loosening up certain rhythmic values, you run the risk of making the rhythms sound like a mistake rather than extra inflections of certain words.

## Respect

Words and Music by
Otis Redding

### *What a Wonderful World* (Weiss and Thiele; as sung by Louis Armstrong)

**The scoop:**  This charming song, made famous by Louis Armstrong, does not span a large range, nor do the dynamics cover a wide spectrum. Nevertheless, be sensitive to the musical shape of each line. The song has an arch in each line of music that gives each line a sense of direction and movement. Be aware of and use the line phrasing to help convey the message of this song.

## What a Wonderful World

Words and Music by
George David Weiss
and Bob Thiele

think _____ to my-self    what a won - der - ful

world. _____    Yes   I    think to my-self

what a won - der - ful    world. _____

### *You Are So Beautiful* (Preston and Fisher; as sung by Joe Cocker)

**The scoop:**   This great song was made popular by the legendary Joe Cocker. The repeated higher notes can pose a problem for some singers, as can the octave jump on the word "everything." With the proper breath support and energy, as well as a working knowledge of how to access the upper range (either head register or falsetto), this song can be sung by either a male or a female. Rhythmically, there are a number of sixteenth-note passages that may cause problems when you first learn the song. If you are sensitive to what you hear in the piano, these passages will make more sense.

# You Are So Beautiful

Words and Music by
Billy Preston and Bruce Fisher

Moderately slow, expressively

### *You Raise Me Up* (Graham and Løvland; as sung by Josh Groban)

**The scoop:** In this modern update of the traditional song "Londonderry Air" (or "Danny Boy"), the singer needs a larger range to encompass all the notes in this piece. This is much easier for a male voice that is comfortable singing in falsetto. As the music goes higher and higher, access to that falsetto will become more and more necessary. However, the song can also be done by a female who can access the lower notes of her range. Although many students may want to sing this song, it may not be right for every voice. It is important for the student and the teacher to assess the capabilities of the student and determine if the singer is ready for the demands of this piece. If the singer can handle the song, *You Raise Me Up,* with its familiar melody, can provide a wonderful learning opportunity.

# You Raise Me Up

Words and Music by
Brendan Graham and Rolf Lovland

When I am down ___ and oh, my soul's so wear-y, when trou-bles

up    to    more    than    I___ can___ be.                        You raise me

up         to    more    than    I___           can___ be.___

## POPULAR STAGE MUSIC

### *Bring Him Home (Les Misérables)*

**The scoop:**    This song is a wonderful ballad from the musical *Les Misérables*. In this song, the large leaps upward can prove difficult for some singers. Remember to sing *through* those top notes, not *to* them. By engaging the breath support and setting the space for the initial vowel *before* you begin to sing, you will find it much easier to sing those leaps successfully. By keeping support engaged throughout, you will be able to provide the high level of emotional intensity required for this song.

# Bring Him Home
## from Les Misérables

Words by
Alain Boublil & Herbert Kretzmer
Music by
Claude-Michel Schönberg

⊕ **CODA**

live._____ Bring him home_____ Bring him

home_____ Bring him home._____

*rit._____*

*dim.*

*pp*

## Give My Regards to Broadway (Little Johnny Jones)

**The scoop:** As with many songs like these by George M. Cohan, take care not to get too caught up in the emotions of the song. It is possible to get so involved in the sheer momentum of these songs that proper singing is treated as an afterthought. Make sure that you have a solid foundation of vocal production under the voice, and *then* have fun with this and other songs like it.

# Give My Regards To Broadway
## from Little Johnny Jones

Geo. M. Cohan

tear - dimmed eye they say good - bye, they're friends with
my name ev - 'ry place you go, as

out a doubt;_____ When the man on the pier_____
town you roam;_____ Wish you'd call on my gal, Now re-

Shouts, "Let them clear," as the ship strikes out._____
mem - ber, old pal, when you get back home._____

Give my re - gards to Broad - way, re-

*p–f*

mem - ber me to Her - ald Square,_____

### *Goodnight, My Someone (The Music Man)*

**The scoop:**   The vocal line in this charming song is fairly simple. It can be hard to keep the initial leap smooth and legato, but after the first leap the melody descends. The range does not get too high. The important thing is to maintain the energy through the descending line. The tendency will be to let the line fizzle out as it gets to a lower, more comfortable part of the vocal range. Avoid allowing this to happen, as the thinness of the accompaniment will make any such vocal issues stand out more.

Goodnight, My Someone
from The Music Man

### *I Cain't Say No (Oklahoma!)*

**The scoop:**   There is really only one issue with this song: it can prove a difficult task to maintain solid vocal production while using a southern drawl (dialect) in singing. Begin by learning this song with a limited amount of drawl so the focus can remain on vocal production. After you have learned the song with a good foundation under it, then you may infuse more drawl at your discretion (and that of your teacher). Remember that this song needs some action! Use this song as an opportunity to really experiment and break out of your shell and comfort zone. Have fun!

I Cain't Say No!
from Oklahoma

Music and Lyrics by
Richard Rodgers and Oscar Hammerstein II

## If I Were a Rich Man (Fiddler on the Roof)

**The scoop:**   This song can be a lot of fun in the hands of the right individual. It is a song that repeats musically but changes the words from verse to verse. The singer is telling a story, so it is important to really express the text while singing. This song does not lend itself to simply standing still and singing. Made famous by the original Tevye, Zero Mostel, this character is larger than life. Your expressions need to reflect his personality.

If I Were a Rich Man
from Fiddler on the Roof

Music by
Jerry Bock
Lyrics by
Sheldon Harnick

## *The Impossible Dream (Man of La Mancha)*

**The scoop:**   Even though this song was written for the male character Don Quixote, on the concert stage this song has been sung successfully by both men and women. At first glance, this song is deceptively simple: the range is confined; the rhythm, although in 9/8, is fairly straightforward. However, the melody continues to build until the singer gets to the section that begins, "This is my quest." This section moves toward the upper part of the range in an inexperienced voice and stays there until the next verse, "And the world." For the student who is first learning this song, it may be beneficial to learn this harder section first and then add the other remaining pages to it. That will help to build up the stamina and energy needed to sing this song successfully.

# The Impossible Dream
## from Man of La Mancha

Music by
Mitch Leigh
Words by
Joe Darion

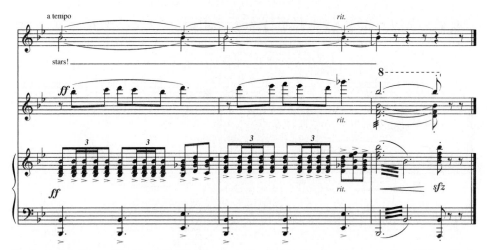

The Impossible Dream (The Quest) by Mitch Leigh and Joe Darion. Reprinted by permission of Helena Music Company/Andrew Scott Music.

## *Johanna (Sweeney Todd)*

**The scoop:**   In this hauntingly pretty song from *Sweeney Todd,* Anthony has just seen Johanna and has fallen in love; however, Johanna is being held captive by the less-than-kind Judge Turpin. Unlike in some songs, where there is a melodic climax and then a tapering-off toward the end, this song continues to build in intensity all the way through the end. In fact, the intensity is then masterfully picked up by the piano and grows until the final chord. This is the musical representation of Anthony's growing determination to follow through with his plan at all costs. Be cautious that the dynamics do not get out of hand while the intensity continues to build. There is a very real danger of giving too much vocally by the end of the song. Although increased dynamics are one way to increase intensity, there are other ways as well, such as crisper diction, accents on certain notes, and even stronger facial expression. Have some fun experimenting in front of a mirror.

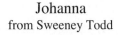

Johanna
from Sweeney Todd

Music and Lyrics by
Stephen Sondheim

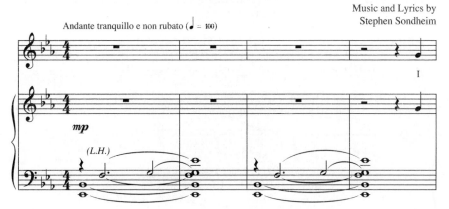

feel you, Jo - han - na, I

feel you. I was half con - vinced I'd wak -

- en, Sat - is - fied e - nough to dream_____ you.

Hap - pi - ly, I was mis - tak - en, Jo - han - na!_____ I

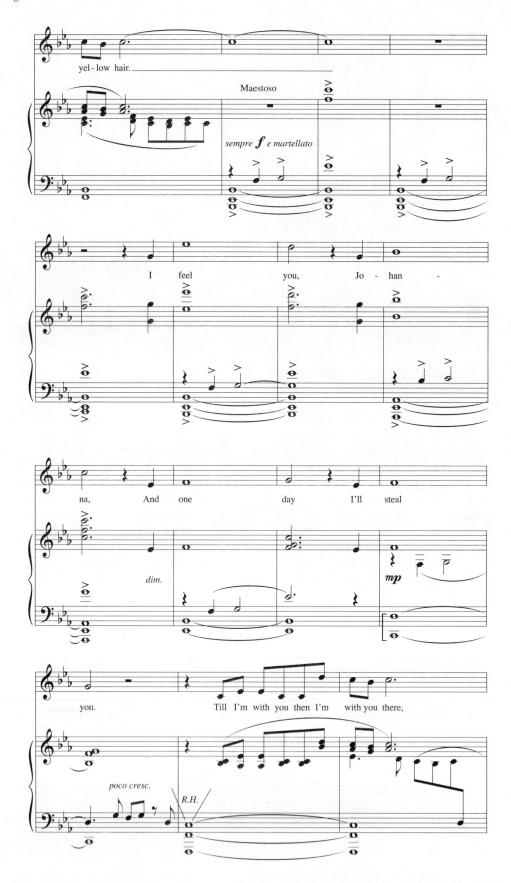

Sweet-ly bur-ied in your yel-low hair.

### June Is Bustin' Out All Over (Carousel)

**The scoop:** At the beginning of this song, there are many accidentals. Make sure that these notes are right in the center of the pitch; otherwise, the song may sound a bit sloppy. The refrain tends to sit on that high E. For each one, make sure that your support is engaged and the space set. The feeling of having the voice higher in the head would be beneficial at this point. This is especially true for the notes that are held longer. Keep the breath energy spinning throughout the duration of the note.

### June Is Bustin' Out All Over
from Carousel

Music and Lyrics by
Rodgers and Hammerstein

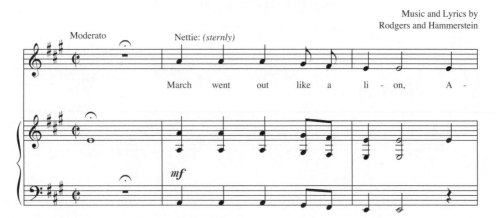

March went out like a li - on, A-

whip-pin' up the wa - ter in the bay. Then Ap - ril cried And

stepped a - side And a - long come pret - ty lit - tle May!

May was full of prom-is - es But she did - n't keep 'em quick e - nough fer

some, And a crowd of Doubt - in' Thom-as - es Was pre -

## Memory (Cats)

**The scoop:** The biggest issue students seem to have with this song is how to sing the rather short, broken-up notes. As with the other songs in this anthology, it is important to constantly strive for a vocal line that is interesting while maintaining a smooth fluidity of line from note to note. Rhythmic precision is necessary and commendable, but it should not be taken to the extreme if it means sacrificing the beautiful, haunting melody that has become a significant part of the American musical theater tapestry.

# Memory
## from Cats

Music by Andrew Lloyd Webber
Text by Trevor Nunn after T. S. Eliot
Arranged by Eric Baumgartner

mut - ters\_\_\_\_ and a street lamp gut - ters\_\_\_\_ and

soon it will be morn - ing. _____

*dim.*

Day - light. _____ I must wait for the sun - rise, \_\_\_\_\_

*mp*

\_ I must think of a new life and I must - n't give

in. _____ When the dawn comes to -

night will be a mem - o - ry too, _____ and a

new day _____ will be - gin.

### *My Funny Valentine (Babes in Arms)*

**The scoop:**    This popular ballad presents an interesting problem that has yet to arise in any other song of the anthology. The entire first part of the song is sung without any piano underneath the voice. On the accompaniment CD, the piano plays the part with the voice, but if you are using a live accompanist, make sure to keep each pitch of the melody energized. This will help keep the vocal line in tune. Strive for the proper note on the word, "You're," when the piano finally joins the voice. If this note is not right in tune, any mistakes in pitch will become immediately evident. With plenty of practice, this beginning section will not be as daunting as it may seem at first.

My Funny Valentine
from Babes in Arms

Music and Lyrics by
Richard Rodgers and Lorenz Hart

SUSIE:

Be - hold the way our fine feath-ered friend his vir - tue doth pa -

don't change a hair for me, Not if you are for me.

More freely

Stay, lit - tle val - en -tine, stay! _____

Slower

Each day is Val - en-tine's day.

*(on cut off)*

*attacca*

Copyright © 1937 by Chappell & Co. Inc.

## *On My Own (Les Misérables)*

**The scoop:** With the international success of *Les Misérables,* this song has easily become the most requested song in my voice classes. Though it has a beautiful melody, it starts quite low in the female range. Because of this fact, as the vocal line rises with each verse, students tend to move more toward a more pop-music, belting sound. Although this song goes high enough to allow the singer to "belt," that practice should be avoided. Approach this music with the same healthy vocal production you would use with any other song in this anthology.

# On My Own
## from Les Misérables

Music by
Claude-michel Schonberg
Lyrics by
Alain Boublil, John Caird, Trevor Nunn,
Jean-marc Natel, and Herbert Kretzmer

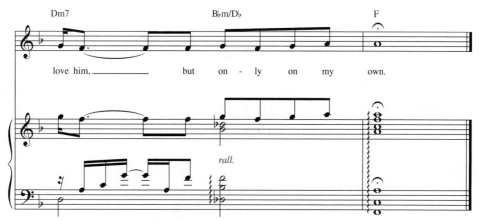

## Over the Rainbow (The Wizard of Oz)

**The scoop:**  It is fairly easy to keep a vocal line smooth and connected when the notes are written stepwise, but how do you keep a line smooth when the most important parts of the melody are larger leaps? That is the question with this song. The main theme is based on larger leaps and descending phrases that musically represent the rainbow that is at the center of the song. The way to keep the line smooth and connected is to keep the direction of the music moving to the end of each sentence. Even though there is a natural stopping point after the first four measures of each sentence, if you think about the vocal line moving to the end of the sentence, the beautiful, melodic arch that has been written into the music will keep the line from sounding choppy.

## Over The Rainbow
from The Wizard of Oz

Music by
Harold Arlen
Lyric by
E.Y. Harburg

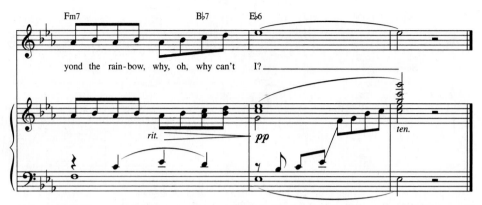

yond the rain-bow, why, oh, why can't I?

## Some Enchanted Evening (South Pacific)

**The scoop:** This song's melody can be described with a couple of single-word descriptions, such as *entrancing* or *enchanting*. Because the line has an almost hypnotic feel as it moves up and down in a short span of time, you need to keep from accenting any of the moving lines. Any "enchantment" that takes place during the moving melody line is meant to be subtle. Calling attention to the melody will make the music seem out of place. Think of this song as a serenade to a love who is not right there to hear it. It is a serenade that is sung with the voice but heard only by the singer's heart.

### Some Enchanted Evening
from South Pacific

Words and Music by
Richard Rodgers and Oscar Hammerstein II

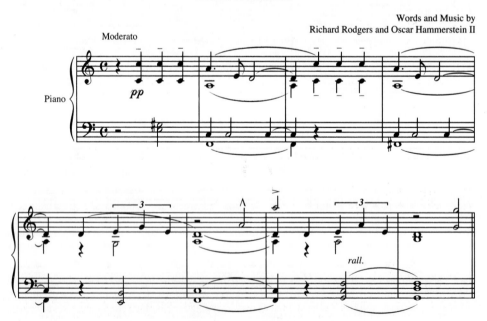

### *Someone to Watch Over Me (Oh, Kay!)*

**The scoop:**   Although individual issues may arise in this song, from student to student, the only big issue that appears with any consistency concerns some of the rhythms. The dotted rhythm that permeates the musical texture of this piece can get a bit too abrupt. If that happens, the line sounds almost clipped off. Make sure to give the full value to each note. Additionally, during the chorus, the syncopated notes that occur at the beginning of each measure, after the initial dotted rhythm, also frequently get to be too rushed. This places unnecessary focus on one or two notes, rather than on the line as a whole. Practice these measures to make sure that the rhythms are solid and precise before you start singing through the song as a whole.

Someone To Watch Over Me
from Oh, Kay!

Music and Lyrics by
George Gershwin and
Ira Gershwin

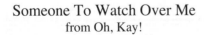

Moderato

There's a say-ing old says that love is blind, still we're of-ten told, "Seek and

ye shall find." So I'm going to seek a cer tain lad I've had in mind.

Look-ing ev-'ry-where, have-n't found him yet; he's the big af-fair I can-

man some girls think of as hand some. To my heart, he car-ries the

key._____ Won't you tell him, please, to put on some speed,

fol-low my lead, oh, how I need some-one to watch o - ver

### Summertime (Porgy and Bess)

**The scoop:**  This aria, like the preceding song, is also by Gershwin. Because of Gershwin's musical language, this aria has the same dotted rhythms and syncopated beats that are found in "Someone to Watch Over Me." However, in this aria, more emphasis is placed on the text, as this is part of an opera. Rather than being a reflective song, like "Someone to Watch Over Me," this aria moves the story forward. That shift in emotion allows the singer to accent some of the notes to emphasize the text. However, any accents must remain tasteful and true to the music that Gershwin wrote.

Summertime
from Porgy and Bess

By George Gershwin,
Du Bose and Dorothy Heyward,
and Ira Gershwin

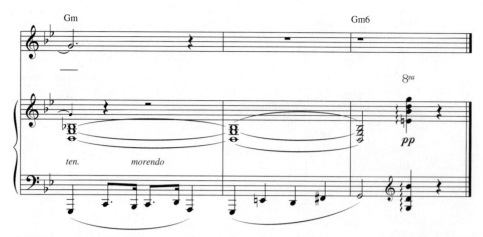

## We Need a Little Christmas (Mame)

**The scoop:** This song is lower than many of the others. Do not try to force the sound to be large and loud in the lower part of your range. The sound will naturally be softer because of the location of the note in the voice. If you try to manipulate the sound to make it louder, it will only make hitting the notes more difficult. Keeping the breath energy engaged throughout this song will make the lower notes work well while still allowing you to have fun with this very popular Christmas song.

### We Need A Little Christmas
from Mame

Music by
Jerry Harman

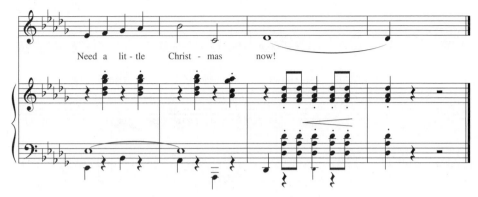

## CLASSICAL MUSIC/ART SONGS

### *Amarilli* (Caccini)

**The scoop:** In this song, the very first note is held for a full measure. Take care that the voice and support are engaged *before* you make any sound. If you try to open your mouth and engage your support as you sing the first note, the first beat or two of music will suffer. This holds true for every time that same held-note passage returns in the music.

Amarilli

Edited by
Horatio Parker

Giulio Caccini
(1546)

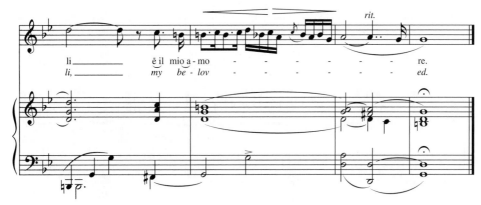

## Beauteous Night, O Night of Love (The Tales of Hoffman)

**The scoop:**    This is a delightful arrangement of the famous barcarolle from *The Tales of Hoffman.* The difference is that in the opera this barcarolle is a duet, whereas here it appears as a solo. You may find it beneficial to feel the music in two bigger beats (i.e., **1**-2-3-**4**-5-6). Although it is necessary to count the six beats in each measure, the smooth melodic line will be easier to sing if you feel the two larger beats. Also, note that all the final "ahs" start with eighth notes. Some students may mistakenly sing quarter notes at first. This is easily corrected.

### Beauteous Night, O Night of Love
(Belle Nuit, Ô Nuit D'Amour)
from The Tales of Hoffman

Translated by
Samuel Richards Gaines

Jacques Offenbach

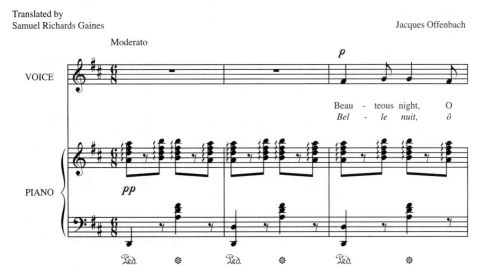

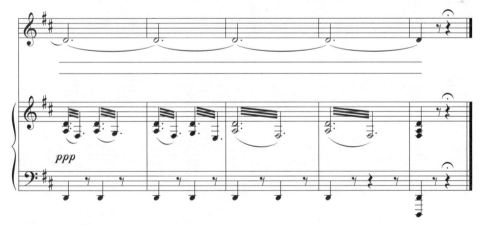

Copyright MCMIX by Oliver Ditson Company.

### *Cradle Song* (Brahms)

**The scoop:**   This song is arguably one of the most famous lullabies ever written. Even if you know this tune already, it is important to work through the music and make sure the notes and rhythms are accurate. Additionally, you will notice that the sense of beat that occurs when singing this song without an accompaniment is lost when the piano joins the voice. With practice, you will find that the song does in fact make sense, even if at first the song with the piano seems impossible.

Cradle Song
(Wiegenlied)
High Voice

Karl Simrock
Translated by Arthur Westbrook

Johannes Brahms, OP. 49, NO. 4

fear. They will guard thee from harm With fair dream-land's sweet
*Baum: Schlaf' nun se - lig und süss, schau' im Traum's Pa - ra*

charm, They will guard thee from harm With fair dream-land's sweet charm.
*dies, schlaf' nun se - lig und süss, schau' im Traum's Pa - ra - dies.*

# Cradle Song
## (Wiegenlied)
### Low Voice

Karl Simrock
Translated by Arthur Westbrook

Johannes Brahms, OP. 49, NO. 4

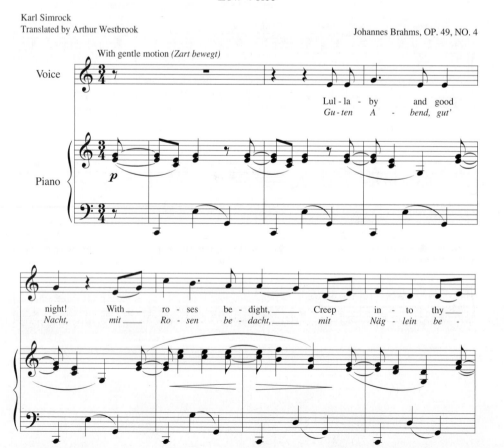

Lul - la - by and good
*Gu - ten A - bend, gut'*

night! With ___ ro - ses be - dight, ___ Creep in - to thy ___
*Nacht, mit ___ Ro - sen be - dacht, ___ mit Näg - lein be -*

bed, There ___ pil - low thy head. If God will, thou shalt
*steckt schlupf' un - ter die Deck: Mor-gen früh, wenn Gott*

wake when the morn - ing doth break, If God will, thou shalt
*will, wirst du wie - der ge - weckt, mor-gen früh, wenn Gott*

wake when the morn - ing doth break.
*will, wirst du wie - der ge - weckt.*

Lul - la - by and good night; Those blue eyes close
*Gu - ten A - bend, gut' Nacht, von ___ Eng' - lein be -*

tight;_____ Bright an - gels are___ near, So sleep with - out
*wacht,_____ die___ zei - gen im___ Traum dir___ Christ - kind - leins*

fear. They will guard thee from harm With fair dream - land's sweet
*Baum: Schlaf' nun se - lig und süss, schau' im Traum's Pa - ra -*

charm, They will guard thee from harm With fair dream - land's sweet charm.
*dies, schlaf' nun se - lig und süss, schau' im Traum's Pa - ra - dies.*

### *Der Vogelfänger bin ich ja (Die Zauberflöte)*

**The scoop:** In Mozart's *Die Zauberflöte (The Magic Flute),* Papageno is a bird catcher who enjoys the simple things in life. This aria occurs at the beginning of the opera when we first meet this beloved character. There are three verses in this aria; however, the only thing that changes is the words. Because of that, the aria must be sung with energy and support, to ensure that listeners do not get bored by hearing the same music over and over. You can have a great deal of fun in conveying this charming aria. Experiment and enjoy!

# Der Vogelfänger bin ich ja
## from Die Zauberflöte

W. A. Mozart

1. Der Vo-gel-fän - ger bin ich ja, stets lu-stig hei sa hop-sa-sa! ich
2. Der Vo-gel-fän - ger bin ich ja, stets lu-stig hei sa hop-sa-sa! ich
3. Wenn al - le Mäd chen wä-ren mein, so tallsch-te ich brav Zu-cker ein, die,

Vo - gel - fän - ger    bin be-kannt    bei    Alt    und Jung im    gan - zen Land.
Vo - gel - fän - ger    bin be-kannt    bei    Alt    und Jung im    gan - zen Land.
wel - che    mir    am    liebsten wär',    der gäb'    ich gleich den    Zu - cker her.

Weiss mit dem Lo - cken    um-zugehn, und mich    auf's Pfeifen zu versteh'n!
Ein Netz für Mädchen    möch-te ich. ich fing'    sie    dutzend -weis' für    mich!
Und kiiss_te    sie    mich    zärtlich daun, wär'    sie    mein Weib und ich ihr Mann.

D'rum kann    ich froh und    lu_stig sein, denn    al - le Vö - gel
Dann sperr-te    ich sie    bei mir ein, und    al - le Mädchen
Sie schlief an    mei-ner    Sei_te ein, ich    wieg-te wie ein

sind    ja    mein.
wä - ren mein.
Kind    sie    ein.

Edition Peters.

## *Drink to Me Only* (Anonymous)

**The scoop:** The melody to this song is almost hymn-like in style. It is a short song with short, four-bar phrases. It is important to give each phrase a sense of motion and direction, or the song as a whole will get tedious and dull. You may also find the 6/8 time signature easier to deal with if you think of the two larger beats in each measure (for example, **1**-2-3 **4**-5-6).

Drink To Me Only

Copyright MCMII by The John Church Company. International copyright secured.

### *Ein Ton* (Cornelius)

**The scoop:**    Upon first review of the music, even students who do not speak German will be able to discern what the title means. The vocal line consists of one note. That can make the song rather boring. However, what the singer does with that note and how the accompaniment is handled can make this a charming song for a student with a limited range. It is important to keep the rhythms precise. It is also important to use the words to determine where the direction of each line goes.

## Ein Ton
### (One Note)

Words and Music by
Peter Cornelius
Eng. Version by J. Ahrem

## *Ich liebe dich* (Beethoven)

**The scoop:** This is a charming song by one of the greatest composers who ever lived. This song simply expresses the emotions of the singer as he or she sings to a loved one. The hard part of the song comes at the end, with the repeated high notes. Be sure to keep the breath energy moving through this part of the song especially, or the tendency will be to close the throat and attempt to control the voice with the neck muscles.

### I Love Thee

Edited by
Horatio Parker

Ludwig Van
Beethoven

shel-ter thee, what-e'er be-fall, And give Love's full-est meas-ure. God shel-ter thee, my

life, my all, O thou, my heart's best treas-ure! O thou, my life's best

treas-ure! My heart's best treas - ure!

## *Le Violette* (Scarlatti)

**The scoop:** The challenge of this song comes from the quick tempo and the separated vocal line. The song should not be taken too fast, or the melody and the words will become unclear. With regard to the vocal line, the song begins with a very nice ascending and descending melodic line; then there is a pause for a couple of beats before the next word is sung. This separation is repeated for the next word. It is this separation that should keep your concentration intact. If you begin to "space out" or forget to count, the rhythmic values of the melody can get tricky.

# Le Violette
### *(The Violet)*

A. Scarlatti.

Ru - gia - do - se,   o - do-
*Sweet - est per-fume fills the*

rose,        vi - o - let-te       gra - zi - o - se                     Rugia - do-se, o - do-
*hours,   'Tis thy   off'ring,   best of  flow-ers,                  Mod -est vio -let, 'tis thy*

ro - se, vi - o -te gra-zi - o - se, vi - o -let - te gra-zi - o - se, Voi vi sta te ver-go-
*treas-ure, Giv - en   to us with - out  meas-ure, Giv - en   to   us with-out   meas -ure, Ah, that we  a  les -son*

gnose           mezzo ascose         mezzo asco - se fra le  foglie,  e sgri - da - te
*learning,      From thy low - ly,   from  thy low-ly, mod-est blooming, All life's weary*

le mie vo -glie        che son tropp'  ambizi -o -se                        e sgridate
*ways perfuming,       All  its false  ambitions spurning,                 All life's weary*

vo - glie, che son tropp' am - bi - zi - o - se          e sgri - da - te le mie
*fum - ing, All its false am - bi -tions spurning,*          *All life's wea - ry way per -*

vo - glie, che son trop - po, son tropp' am - bi - zi - o - se.          Ru - gia -
*fum - ing, All its false, yes, its false am - bi - tion spurning.*          *Sweet-est*

do - se o - do - ro - se          vi - o - let -te, vi - o - let -te, gra - zi - o - se,
*per-fume fills the hours,*          *'Tis thy off 'ring, best of flow -ers, best of flow-ers.*

ru - gia - do - se,          o - do - ro - se, vi - o - let -te, vi - o - let -te gra -zi - o -
*Love - ly vio - let,*          *mod - est bloom -ing, I would greet thee, dear-est, best of all the flow-*

se, vi - o - let -te, vi - o - let -te gra - zi - o - - - se!
*ers, Mod -est vio - let, love-ly flow - er, love - ly flow - - er!*

### *Little Karen* (Heise)

**The scoop:**   This song is a conversation with a person who is supposedly present while you are singing. The first part of each verse reflects on events that have already taken place; the last part of each verse contains a small refrain that poses a question to Little Karen. When performing this song, find one point in the room and sing to it in an attempt to convey the location of Little Karen. Without that focal point on the singer's part, the idea of a discussion will be lost on the listener.

Little Karen†

P. Heise

1. Dost remem-ber, dear, when last Au-tumn home we went   Thro' the fields, how
2. Dost remem-ber, too, when a-round the hearth sat we,   Thou didst si-lent

oft thy blue eyes on me were bent?   It flash'd a-cross my mind That till
list to the sto-ries told by me?   Thy gaze on me was turn'd, Till my

then   I had been   blind,   Tell me, lit-tle   Kar-en, what thy   heart felt
heart with-in me   burn'd,   Tell me, lit-tle   Kar-en, what thy   heart felt

then,   Tell me, lit-tle   Kar-en, what thy   heart felt   then?
then,   Tell me, lit-tle   Kar-en, what thy   heart felt   then?

† Pronounce the *a* broadly, as in the word *far*.

The lyrics under the musical staves:

3. When at Christmas-tide, to the mu-sic's cheer-ful sound, We with nim-ble
4. Now the Spring is here, see, the buds are o-p'ning wide, Birds be-gin to

feet flit-ted gai-ly o'er the ground; I glanc'd but did not speak, Deep
build, na-ture's deck'd now like a bride; All things that live and move Are

crim-son grew thy cheek, Tell me, lit-tle Kar-en, what thy heart felt
dreaming but of love, Tell me, lit-tle Kar-en, what thy heart feels

then, Tell me, lit-tle Kar-en, what 'thy heart felt 'then?
now, Tell me, lit-tle Kar-en, what thy heart feels now?

### *Mattinata* (Tosti)

**The scoop:**   This song is a wonderful salute to the morning. Though not subtle or un-derstated in tone, the song slowly signals the end of night and the upcoming morning. There is one spot to watch out for: In the verse that begins "My only pray'r," the tonality changes slightly. Beginning singers will have already gotten used to the melody that ap-pears in verses one and two, so this quick change may take some mental adjustment.

# Matin Song

Enrico Panzacchi
Translated by Isidora Martinez

F. Paolo Tosti

In lu-cent bil - low A dream of heav'n - ly sphere!

Ma - ry,_____ the last star fail - ing_____ In deep-est

az - ure Full soon will fade a - way._____

### *My Mother Loves Me Not* (Brahms)

**The scoop:** This short, melancholy song is very expressive. Maintain a smooth, flowing musical line while striving to really enunciate the text. As this song is in three small verses, the mood that the text conveys is lost if the listener cannot understand the words.

My Mother Loves Me Not

High Voice

Volkslied
(Swabian Folksong)
Translated by E. D'Esterre-Keeling

Johannes Brahms, Op. 7, No. 5

# My Mother Loves Me Not
## Low Voice

Volkslied
(Swabian Folksong)
Translated by E. D'Esterre-Keeling

Johannes Brahms, Op. 7, No. 5

1. My moth-er loves me not, An' no sweet-heart ha' I got;
2. Look! how the oth-ers dance, I nev-er get a chance.

Eh, why do I not die? What use am I?
Ev'n if I would dance now, I don't know how.

3. Let the three ro-ses blow

That by yon cross do grow: Knew ye, per-chance, the maid Who there is laid?

Copyright © 1854 by Oliver Ditson Company.

### *Nina* (Pergolesi)

**The scoop:** Even though this song is traditionally sung by a male, a female can sing it just as well. The key presented here is a bit high for most beginning male singers, but if a male would like to attempt to sing this, he should sing the high notes in falsetto until he has gained access to the head register. Also note that the ascending line to the high G must be worked and practiced with proper support and vertical space. Do not try to give as much sound on the top note as you feel on the bottom note. This will only create vocal problems and bad habits.

## Nina

Edited by
Horatio Parker

G. B. Pergolesi

### *None But the Lonely Heart* (Tchaikovsky)

**The scoop:** This text, by Goethe, has been set by a number of composers. Tchaikovsky is known for his haunting melodies. Because of that, you will need to maintain a smooth and legato musical line throughout the song. Additionally, the piano has a syncopated pattern that may pose quite a challenge to some beginning singers. You will find success in navigating the syncopations if you listen to the right hand during the introduction. There the vocal line is played against the syncopation, so you can hear how the parts line up together.

## None But The Lonely Heart
### High Voice

Johann Wolfgang von Goethe (1749–1832)
Translated By Arthur Westbrook

Peter Ilyitch Tchaikovsky., Op. 6, No. 6

Andante non tanto.

# None But The Lonely Heart
## Low Voice

Johann Wolfgang von Goethe
Translated by Arthur Westbrook

Peter Ilyitch Tchaikovsky., Op. 6, No. 6

### *The Sea* (MacDowell)

**The scoop:**   Even though the music is in 6/8, it is the strong beats on one and four that give this song the sense of rocking with the ocean waves. The large rise and fall in the vocal line further adds to the idea of the waves of the sea. The difficult part of this song comes during the climax of each verse, where the voice is near the top of its range and is asked to drop a full octave before returning to the higher note. Make sure to keep the air spinning through the top note while not giving too much vocal weight to the lower note. It happens fast enough that if you try to get a big sound on the brief lower note, it will be extremely difficult to return to the upper note. By decreasing the vocal size of the lower, quicker note, you can maintain the space and energy of the top notes and simply return to that space as the line moves back up.

## The Sea

William Dean Howells

Edward A. Macdowell, Op. 47, No. 7

### *Voi, che sapete (Le Nozze di Figaro)*

**The scoop:** The teenage boy, Cherubino, is dressed in full military uniform, ready to go off to battle. However, he is experiencing some new feelings about the opposite sex. He sings this aria to all the ladies who are listening, in an attempt to determine if this is love. This aria is sung by a female, as the role of Cherubino is what we call a *pants role* (or *breeches role*); literally, that is the role of a male character sung by a female. The music is fun, as Cherubino expresses all the different sensations and feelings he is experiencing. Any student who sings this aria should be sensitive to the fact that she is playing a member of the opposite sex. Take care not to overact at the expense of the charming melody that Mozart has written. Remember, it is the music that separates an aria from a theatrical monologue.

# Voi, che sapete
## from Le nozze di Figaro

W. A. Mozart

# INTERNATIONAL SONGS

## *The Ash Grove* (Wales)

**The scoop:** The music for this song has also found its way into hymns. It is a popular song in which the piano mimics the sounds of the harp that is referred to in the first verse. Be sensitive to the arch of each musical line. The rise and fall of the music gives the singer a visual idea of the direction of each phrase, with the swell on the ascending part of the line and the taper on the descending part.

The Ash Grove
(Wales)

Translated by John Oxenford

Old Melody
Edited and arranged by Granville Bantock

1. The ash grove how grace-ful, how plain-ly 'tis speak-ing, The
2. My lips smile no more, my heart los-es its light-ness, No

harp thro' it play-ing has lan-guage for me; When-ev-er the light 'thro its
dream of the fu-ture my spir-it can cheer, I on-ly would brood on the

branch-es is break-ing, A host of kind fa-ces is gaz-ing on me. The
past and its bright-ness, The dead I have mourn'd are a-gain liv-ing here. From

friends of my child-hood a - gain are be - fore me, Each step wakes a
ev' - ry dark nook they press for - ward to meet me, I lift up my

mem - 'ry, as free - ly I roam, With soft whis - pers la - den, its
eyes to the broad leaf - y dome, And oth - ers are there look - ing

leaves rus - tle o'er me, The ash grove, the ash grove a - lone is my home.
down-ward to greet me, The ash grove, the ash grove a - lone is my home.

Copyright MCMXI by Oliver Ditson Company.

### *The Fair Maid of Sorrento* (Italy)

**The scoop:**   Only the English version of this song is presented here, because the text
of this folk song from Naples was originally written in the Neapolitan dialect. Because
of the differences between traditional Italian and the Neapolitan dialect, I chose the
English to minimize any confusion with other Italian songs in this anthology. Maintain
a sense of smooth continuity while singing to convey the fond memories and yearning
emotion of each line.

# The Fair Maid of Sorrento

## (Italy [*Naples*])

Translated by H. F. B.

Folksong
Edited and arranged by Granville Bantock

1. Sweet thine eyes at___ Pie - di - grot-ta, Fill'd my soul with___ soft de-
2. Peace for - ev - er___ has de - part-ed, Night and day my___ strength is

sir-ing, Trip-ping light-ly,___ by thy moth-er, Pearls and gold were___ thy at-
fail-ing, Then the rud-der___ help-less leav-ing, To the great sea___ am I

tir-ing. Laced with gold was___ all thy ves-ture, Silk - en ker-chief___ shin-ing
sail-ing. Wretch-ed ves - sel,___ wild waves leap-ing, Towards Sor - ren - to___ swift-ly

un - der, With a sweet-ly___ 'witch-ing ges-ture, Didst thou laugh then___ joy - ous-
bear thee, I in twi-light___ shades am weep-ing, Does she hear my___ lone - ly

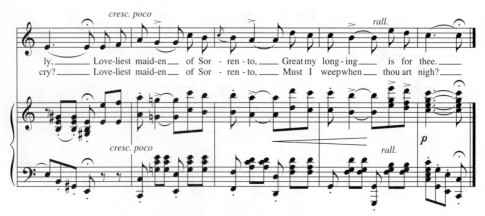

### *Yo m'alegro de habèr sido [If 'Tis Sorrow So to Love Thee]* (Spain)

**The scoop:**   This song can be sung as a solo or a duet. If sung as a duet, each singer should realize that the parts move together in close relationship. When it is sung as a solo, the student should be ready for the rhythmic patterns that are held over to the next measure. This will blur the line between beats. Counting is a priority through these sections. Also, the upper voice, which is the melody, does soar a bit high. You will do well to maintain long, vertical vowels and plenty of breath support through each of the higher notes.

### *The Last Rose of Summer* (Ireland)

**The scoop:**   This popular song presents one technical issue a number of times with each verse. There is a large leap after the first part of each phrase. Maintain a nice arch up and over that higher note to keep the smooth legato quality of the melody. Students tend to hit the upper note with a bit too much force, which causes that one note to stick out in the context of the melody. Work to keep the line smooth.

## The Last Rose of Summer
### (Ireland)

Air: The Groves of Blarney
Edited and Arranged by Granville Bantock

Thomas Moore (1779–1852)

rose - bud is nigh, ____To re - flect back her__blush-es Or__ give sigh for__ sigh.
leaves____ o'er the bed, ___Where thy mates of__the__ gar-den Lie__ scent - less and__ dead.

## *Loch Lomond* (Scotland)

**The scoop:**  This famous song has three verses plus a refrain. It is important to maintain the emotion and energy throughout the verses. Sometimes students have a tendency to sing through the verses without much energy but then infuse a wave of emotions once the popular refrain begins. This makes the song sound uneven and lopsided. Also, the words need to remain consistent throughout. If you decide to modify some of the text in the song to more traditional pronunciations, take care to modify *all* of the different words. Maintaining consistency in all aspects of the song is the key to success with this piece.

### Loch Lomond.
*(The bonnie banks o' Loch Lomon')*

Jacobite Air

1. By    yon bon-nie banks    and    yon bon-nie braes, Where the    sun shines bright on Loch
2. The    wee bird-ies sing an' the    wild flow-ers spring, An' in    sun-shine the    wa - ters are

## *Cancion de Mayo [May Song]* (Spain)

**The scoop:** In this shorter song from Spain, you will need to be aware of the runs that are present throughout. For the most part, the runs are small and contain only a few notes. However, a look at the ending of the song reveals a large run that continues through to the end. The run begins as an ascending and descending pattern with a slight repeat toward the top of the line. The run then ends with a written two-note repetition that is more of a slow, trill-like passage. The goal should be to sing this run in one breath, but if that is not possible, wait until the end of a pattern before interrupting the line and taking a breath.

May Song
(Cancion De Maja)
(Spain)

vails your \_\_\_ pain. All your wiles ig-nor - ing, Free as bird I'm soar - ing, All your sweet al-
*o - ca - sion? A - si di ma-jo - ta Quie-ro siem-pre an-dar, \_\_\_ Que\_esel ma-ne-*

lure - ments Light-ly I dis - dain, \_\_\_ Gay I'm sing - ing, "Go, poor lov-ers, \_\_\_
*ji - llo De der-ra-mar sal, \_\_\_ Y yo le di - go; Ar - ri - ma-te\_\_\_*

come not \_\_\_ near, \_\_\_ Go, poor lov-ers, \_\_\_ come not \_\_\_ near." Ah \_\_\_
*pa - ra\_a \_\_\_ llá, \_\_\_ Ar - ri - ma-te\_\_\_ pa - ra\_a - llà. Ay! \_\_\_*

## *O Tannenbaum [O Faithful Pine]* (Germany)

**The scoop:** The first verse of this song is part of the traditional Christmas carol. The second verse is part of a folk song that is not the famous carol. The danger of this version of the song comes with the overwhelming familiarity of the Christmas carol. This song must be approached like an art song, with proper attention given to vocal production, diction, and phrasing. Resist the urge to break into an unsupported caroling mode when learning this song.

O Faithful Pine

(O Tannenbaum)

(Germany)

Adapted by August Zarnock (1819)
Translated By H.F.B.

Westphalian Folksong
Edited and Arranged By Granville Bantock

1. O faith-ful pine, O faith-ful pine, Green are thy leaves for-ev - er!
1. O Tan-nen-baum, O Tan-nen-baum, Wie treu sind dei-ne Blät - ter!

Not on - ly green in sum-mer's prime, But in the snow - y
Du grünst nicht nur zur Som-mer - zeit, Nein, auch in Win - ter

win - ter - time! O faith-ful pine, O faith-ful pine, Green are thy leaves for - ev - er!
wenn es schneit. O Tan-nen-baum, O Tan-nen-baum, Wie treu sind dei - ne Blät - ter!

2. The night-in-gale, the night-in-gale You took for your ex - am - ple!
2. *Die Nach-ti-gall, die Nach-ti-gall Nahmst du dir zum Ex - em - pel!*

She sings in sum - mer all the day, But flies when falls the
*Sie bleibt so lang der Som-mer lacht, Im Herbst sie sich von*

au-tumn gray. The night-in-gale, the night-in-gale You took for your ex - am - ple!
*dan-nen macht. Die Nach-ti-gall, die Nach-ti-gall Nahmst du dir zum Ex - em - pel!*

### *A un niño ciegocito [Unto a Poor Blind Lover]* (Spain)

**The scoop:**    As with the other song from Spain, this song contains a couple of tricky runs, only this time the rhythms in each run are a little more difficult. Learn the runs slowly and precisely first. Then, as you get more proficient with the notes and rhythms of each run, you can increase the speed. Additionally, as with the other song, if you cannot successfully complete the run in one breath, wait until the end of a pattern before taking a breath in the mddle of the run.

# Unto A Poor Blind Lover
## (A Un Niño Ciegocito)
### Bolero
#### (Spain)

Translated by H.F.B.

Folksong
Edited and Arranged by Granville Bantock

# DUETS

## *All I Ask of You (Phantom of the Opera)*

**The scoop:**   This is a famous, but rather difficult, duet that has become quite popular at weddings. Students who are interested in singing this duet must take care when singing in the extremes of the vocal range. At the beginning of each verse, the part that starts the verse is singing alone and the music is softer. There is no need to try and shake the roof by oversinging. Then, once both voices join forces toward the end of the duet, the tendency will be to try to sing over the other person. Remember that if you cannot hear yourself when next to another singer, find someone to listen to the rehearsal and check the balance. Any oversinging that occurs in the attempt to compensate for the inability to hear oneself will lead to vocal fatigue at best and vocal damage at worst.

All I Ask of You
from The Phantom of the Opera

Music by Andrew Lloyd Webber
Lyrics by Charles Hart
Additional Lyrics by Richard Stilgoe

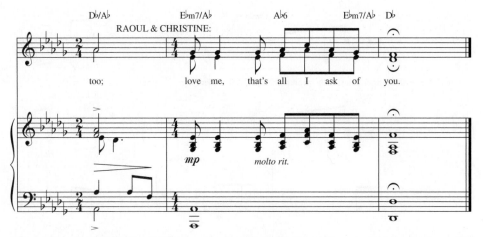

### *Anything You Can Do (Annie Get Your Gun)*

**The scoop:**    The difficulty in this duet comes from the sheer speed of the music. It is a playful banter between Annie and Frank. It is important to practice this duet slowly at first, and allow the speed to come as each person becomes familiar and comfortable with the music. The other pitfall of this duet is when Annie boasts that she can hold a note longer than Frank—and then does. Make sure to take a *large* breath right before the final "Yes I," before the held note. If you miss that breath, there is virtually no way to successfully hold the note as long as written. Also, you will have to work up to holding the note that long. Do not expect to be able to hold the note for as long as written on the first attempt. It will take practice.

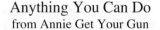

Anything You Can Do
from Annie Get Your Gun

Words and Music by
Irving Berlin

### *People Will Say We're in Love (Oklahoma!)*

**The scoop:**    This charming duet from *Oklahoma!* is different from the other duets in this anthology in one significant way: It is the only duet in which the two voices do not ever sing together. The parts relate to each other and talk to each other, but each voice takes its own verse. Although the music does not venture too high or low for either voice, each singer should make sure to save plenty of energy and support for the last page, where the musical line does go a little higher.

## People Will Say We're In Love
from Oklahoma

Words and Lyrics by
Richard Rodgers and Oscar Hammerstein II

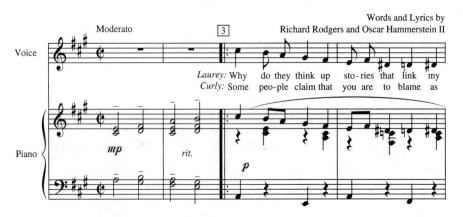

glove. _____ Sweet - heart _____ they're sus -
bove. _____ They'll see _____ it's al -

pect - ing things _____ Peo - ple will say we're in
right with me _____ Peo - ple will say we're in

love. _____ love. _____

### *The Prayer* (Foster and Bayer Sager; as sung by Celine Dion/Andrea Bocelli)

**The scoop:** This is another duet, like "All I Ask of You," that travels to the extremes of the vocal ranges. The upper voice is asked to explore the depths of the range and the lower voice is asked to soar quite high. Add to that the fact that, at one point, one singer is singing in English while the other is singing in Italian, and you have a rather difficult duet. However, this duet is not insurmountable or impossible. As long as both voices are sensitive to each other and do not turn this song into a contest to see who can be heard better, the music can be successfully navigated once it has been properly learned. It is easy to see why this amazing piece is popular at weddings.

# The Prayer

Words and Music by
Carole Bayer Sager and David Foster
Italian Lyric by
Alberto Testa And Tony Renis

### Wunderbar (Kiss Me, Kate)

**The scoop:**   The final duet of this anthology presents one issue of which each singer should be aware: It uses German words sporadically throughout the song. The first, and most predominant, word is also the title of the duet, the word *Wunderbar*. This word, which means "wonderful," is pronounced with an initial "v" as if the word were spelled VOON-der-bar. The other three words that are borrowed from the German are:

1. *Jungfrau* [one of the famous peaks of the northern Swiss alps]—the first part of the word is pronounced with a *y* instead of a *j* and the second part is pronounced like the word *frown* without the *n* (i.e., YUNG-frow).

2. *Liebchen* [sweetheart]—pronounced like LEAP-yen.

3. *mein* [myn]—pronounced like the English word "mine."

# Wunderbar
## from Kiss Me, Kate

Music and Words by
Cole Porter

favourite star above; _____

What a bright shin - ing

*molto rit.*

Like our love, it's Wun - der - bar!

star! _____ Like our love, it's Wun - der - bar!

*molto rit.*

*p molto rit.*

VERSE
FRED:                                              LILLI:

Gaz - ing down on the Jung - frau        From our se - cret

*a tempo*

FRED: 45                              LILLI

cha- let for two,_____ Let us drink, Lieb-chen mein, In the moon-light be-

FI.

poco rit.        a tempo

nign, To the joy of our dream come true._____

poco rit.        a tempo

To the joy of our dream come true._____

poco rit.   a tempo

Str.

55 REFRAIN

Wun-der - bar,_____ Wun-der - bar!_____

Wun-der - bar,_____ Wun-der - bar!_____ What a

WUNDERBAR (from "Kiss Me Kate"). Words and music by Cole Porter. Copyright © 1952 by Cole Porter. Copyright assigned to John F. Wharton, as Trustee of the Cole Porter Music and Literary Property Trusts. Chappell & Co., Inc. Owner of Publication and Allied Rights Throughout the World. All rights reserved. Used by permission.

# Bibliography

Doscher, Barbara. *The Functional Unity of the Singing Voice.* 2d ed. Lanham, MD: Scarecrow Press, 1994.

Miller, Richard. *The Structure of Singing: System and Art in Vocal Technique.* Belmont, CA: Schirmer/ Thompson Learning, 1996.

Sataloff, Robert T., ed. *Vocal Health and Pedagogy.* Vol. 2, *Advanced Assessment and Treatment,* 2d ed. San Diego: Plural Publishing, 2006.

Sataloff, Robert T. *Voice Science.* San Diego: Plural Publishing, 2005.

# Glossary

**abdominal muscles**—The muscles located in the lower half of the torso between the diaphragm and the pelvis. They assist in the development and use of breath support.

**abduction**—The action of separating the vocal folds to their open and relaxed position.

**adduction**—The action of bringing the vocal folds together in preparation for phonation.

**articulation**—Any type of musical or textual emphasis placed on a note or passage.

**arytenoids**—Two pyramid-shaped cartilages, located in the rear of the larynx, that are attached to the vocal folds. They are responsible for small adjustments in pitch.

**breath markings**—Any type of marking written in music, either by the composer or the singer, to indicate where to take a breath. When added by the composer, they are usually represented by a large comma over the music.

**breath support**—The function of controlling the release of air during exhalation. This is the foundation of any good vocal technique. Without good breath support, healthy singing is not possible.

**bronchioles**—Smaller tubes that branch off from each bronchus. They are part of the pathway by which air gets to and from the lungs.

**bronchus**—One of two large tubes that branch off from the trachea. The *bronchi* (plural) are part of the pathway by which air gets to and from the lungs.

**cadenza**—A musical flourish found at the end of a song or aria before the cadence. This is where the singer demonstrates vocal virtuosity. The additions and embellishments may be written out or invented by the singer.

**chest register**—The part of the overall range of the voice that encompasses the lower notes. It is termed the chest register for the sensations that are felt in the chest when singing in that range. However, it is important to remember that the location of the voice (sound production) does not actually move into the chest.

**crescendo**—A musical articulation that means to get louder (increase volume). This is usually signified by a long, narrow "less-than" sign or the abbreviation "cresc." The plural is *crescendi*.

**cricoid cartilage**—The smaller of the two large cartilages found in the larynx. The large part of this cartilage faces the back of the trachea and is considered the bottom of the larynx.

**decrescendo**—A musical articulation that means to get softer (reduce volume). This is usually signified by a long, narrow "greater-than" sign or the abbreviation "decresc." or "dim." (for *diminuendo*). The plural is *decrescendi*.

**diaphragm**—The large muscle that separates the chest cavity from the abdominal cavity. It is an involuntary muscle that initiates the action of breathing.

**dynamics**—Musical markings that convey to the singer when to get softer or louder.

**epiglottis**—The cartilage that is attached to the interior of the larynx and extends to the top of the trachea. Its function is to close off the trachea when swallowing food or liquid, to keep those things out of the lungs.

**falsetto**—Typically, the uppermost register in the male voice (some argue that there is a falsetto in the female voice as well). It is characterized by a high, almost female-sounding quality.

**focus**—A term used to describe the resonance of the voice. It means the inherent point, or lack thereof, in the sound. The focus gives the voice its natural projection.

**head register**—The part of the overall range of the voice that encompasses the higher notes. It is termed the head register for the sensations that are felt in the head, especially in the sinus area of the face, when singing in that range. However, it is important to remember that the location of the voice (sound production) does not actually move into the head.

**hyoid bone**—The only bone of the larynx. It marks the top of the larynx and attaches at the base of the tongue.

**intercostal muscles**—The muscles that are attached to the ribs. There are two kinds: internal and external. They are responsible for expanding and contracting the rib cage.

**laryngopharynx**—The section of the pharynx that incorporates the space from the larynx to the base of the tongue.

**larynx**—The voice box. It houses the vocal folds and is primarily responsible for the production of sound.

**legato**—A type of musical line that requires each note to be smooth and connected to the next note; it is achieved by maintaining a constant, steady, uninterrupted flow of air throughout the melodic phrase. This is the opposite of a short, choppy, separated, staccato musical line.

**meter**—The time signature of the music. Usually delineated by a time signature at the beginning of the song (e.g., 4/4 or 6/8). The top number of the meter marking tells how many beats there are in a measure. The bottom number tells which note receives one full beat.

**melody**—The primary vocal line in a song.

**middle register**—The part of the overall range of the voice that encompasses the notes in the middle of the range. The middle register is a difficult area for singers because the notes it encompasses can be produced in a number of ways depending on many variables (e.g., dynamics, consonants used, vowel of the word, approach to the note, etc.).

**nasopharynx**—The section of the pharynx that incorporates the space from the roof of the mouth to the nasal cavity.

**octave**—In music theory, an octave is the same note as the first pitch, but higher in the major and minor keys by eight notes. For example, in the key of C major, the scale is C-D-E-F-G-A-B-C. The octave is the two Cs.

**oropharynx**—The section of the pharynx that incorporates the space from the base of the tongue to the roof of the mouth.

**pharynx**—The space behind the nose, mouth, and the beginning of the throat that is used to pass air and food into the appropriate tubes (trachea and esophagus, respectively). It is divided into three sections (laryngo-, oro-, naso-).

**phonation**—The process of making vocal or speech-related sound.

**phrase shaping**—The art of creating a melodic musical line by adding crescendi, decrescendi, movement, and intensity.

**pitch**—The sound of a given note; the wavelength or frequency of vibration of a sound.

**range**—A word that describes how high or low a song goes; also, the span of notes that an individual voice can produce.

**registers**—Sections of the overall range of a voice that are associated with different sensations (for example, head register).

**resonance**—A term used to describe the naturally occurring amplification of the voice or another musical instrument. Resonance contributes to the timbre to give each voice a distinct and unique sound.

**rhythm**—The duration of each musical note and rest in relation to the overall melodic line.

**score mapping**—The process in which a singer makes notes in a score to call attention to each of the different aspects of a melody. This is useful in remembering breaths, dynamics, and other articulations.

**tempo**—Term used to describe how fast or slow a song should be sung.

**thyroid cartilage**—The larger of the two large cartilages found in the larynx. From the side, it looks like a belt with a wide belt buckle, even though it is not connected to itself in the back. The vocal folds are connected to the inside of this cartilage. The rocking movement of the thyroid cartilage, in conjunction with the cricoid cartilage, is responsible for large pitch adjustment.

**timbres**—The inherent colors and tone quality of the voice. The term describes the unique sound of each voice (e.g., "he has a darker timbre to his voice").

**tonic triad**—In music theory, the three notes in the key of the music that are represented by do–mi–sol or 1–3–5.

**trachea**—The windpipe; the main tube that allows air to move from outside of the body into the lungs and vice versa.

**vocal folds**—Two membranes, located in the larynx, that vibrate to create sound.

**vocal nodules**—The equivalent of calluses on the vocal folds, caused by friction. They can form after repeated abuse and/or misuse of the voice.

**vocalise**—A vocal exercise. There are two types of vocalises: basic and advanced. They can be used to warm up the voice or work on a specific vocal issue.

# Song Index

## A

A un niño ciegocito (Bantock, arranger), 290–292
All I Ask of You (Webber), 293–298
Amarilli (Caccini), 231–233
Amazing Grace (traditional), 41
Angels Through the Night (Kern, arranger), 42–49
Anything You Can Do (Berlin), 298–308
The Ash Grove (Bantock, arranger), 279–280
Ave Maria (Schubert), 49–55

## B

Beauteous Night, O Night of Love (Offenbach), 233–237
Beautiful Dreamer (Foster), 72–75
Because (d'Hardelot), 76–80
Bring Him Home (Boublil, Kretzmer, & Schönberg), 257–260

## C

Cancion de Mayo (Bantock, arranger), 287–288
Cradle Song (Brahms), 238–242

## D

Der Vogelfänger bin ich ja (Mozart), 242–244
Dixie (Emmett), 80–82
Dreamy Hawaii (Vandersloot), 82–86
Drink to Me Only (Anonymous), 245–246

## E

Ein Ton (Cornelius), 246–249

## F

The Fair Maid of Sorrento (Bantock, arranger), 280–282

## G

Give My Regards to Broadway (Cohan), 160–164
Goodnight, My Someone (Willson), 164–167

## H

Have You Ever Really Loved a Woman (Kamen), 116–121
How Do I Live (Warren), 122–125

## I

I Cain't Say No (Rodgers & Hammerstein), 168–173
I Walked Today Where Jesus Walked (O'Hara), 56–61
Ich liebe dich (Beethoven), 249–251
If I Were a Rich Man (Harnick & Bock), 173–181
If 'Tis Sorrow So to Love Thee (Bantock, arranger), 282–284
The Impossible Dream (Darion & Leigh), 181–185

## J

Jeanie with the Light Brown Hair (Foster), 86–91
Johanna (Sondheim), 185–189
The John Brown Song (traditional), 91–92
June Is Bustin' Out All Over (Rodgers & Hammerstein), 189–194

## K

Kiss Me, Kate (Porter), 320–328

## L

The Last Rose of Summer (Bantock, arranger), 284–285
Le Violette (Scarlatti), 251–254
Leave Me with a Smile (Koehler & Burtnett), 93–95
Little Karen (Heise), 255–256
Loch Lommond (Scottish traditional), 285
The Lord Is My Shepherd (Kaplan), 61–64

## M

Mattinata (Tosti), 256–261
May Song (Bantock, arranger), 287–288
Memory (Webber & Nunn), 194–198

Minnie, the Moocher (Calloway & Mills), 125–127
M-O-T-H-E-R (Morse), 96–99
My Funny Valentine (Rodgers & Hart), 198–201
My Heart Will Go On (Horner), 127–137
My Mother Loves Me Not (Brahms), 262–263

## N

Nina (Pergolesi), 264–266
None But the Lonely Heart (Tchaikovsky), 266–272

## O

O Faithful Pine (Bantock, arranger), 289–290
The Old Rugged Cross (traditional), 67
On My Own (Boublil, Caird, Nunn, Natel, Kretzmer, & Schonberg), 202–207
O'Tannenbaum (Bantock, arranger), 289–290
Over The Rainbow (Harburg & Arlen), 207–212
Over There (Cohan), 100–102
Oy Hanukkah, Oy Hanukkah (traditional), 65–66

## P

People Will Say We're in Love (Rodgers & Hammerstein), 302–312
The Prayer (Foster & Bayer Sager), 312–320

## R

R-E-S-P-E-C-T (Redding), 138–142

## S

The Sea (MacDowell), 272–274
Smilin' Through (Penn), 102–104
Some Enchanted Evening (Rodgers & Hammerstein), 212–217
Someone to Watch Over Me (Gershwin & Gershwin), 217–222
Star of the East (Kennedy), 68–71

Summertime (Gershwin, Heyward, Heyward, & Gershwin), 222–226

**T**

Tenting on the Old Camp Ground (Kittredge), 104–106

**U**

Unto a Poor Blind Lover (Bantock, arranger), 290–292

**V**

Voi, che sapete (Mozart), 274–278

**W**

We Need a Little Christmas (Harman), 226–231

What a Wonderful World (Weiss & Thiele), 143–147

When I Survey the Wondrous Cross (traditional), 71

Wunderbar (Porter), 320–328

**Y**

The Yankee Doodle Boy (Cohan), 106–111

Yo m'alegro de habèr sido (Bantock, arranger), 282–284

You Are So Beautiful (Preston & Fisher), 147–151

You Raise Me Up (Graham & Løvland), 151–157

You're a Grand Old Flag (Cohan), 112–116

# Subject Index

## A

Abdominal cavity, 7, 8*f*
Abdominal muscles, 8, 10–11
Abduction, 13
Abuse, of voice, 37–38
Accompaniment, 4–5
Adam's apple, 12
Adams, Bryan, 116–121
Adduction, 13
Advent, 68–71
Air, 11
Alcohol, 38
American English, 5
Anatomy
    breath support and, 7–9
    sound production and, 12–16
*Annie Get Your Gun* (play), 298–308
Antihistamines, 38
Arlen, Harold, 207–212
Armstrong, Louis, 143–147
Arytenoids, 12, 13–14, 13*f*

## B

*Babes in Arms* (play), 198–201
Bantock, Granville, 279–285, 287–292
Bayer Sager, Carole, 312–320
Beethoven, Ludwig van, 249–251
Bell, 14
Berlin, Irving, 298–308
Bocelli, Andrea, 312–320
Bock, Jerry, 173–181
Boublil, Alain, 201–207, 257–260
Brahms, Johannes, 238–242, 262–263
Breath location, 30, 31
Breath support
    exercises for, 10–11, 20–21
    overview of, 7, 10
    posture for, 2
    respiratory system and, 7–8
Bronchiole, 7, 8*f*
Bronchus, 7, 8*f*
Burtnett, Earl, 93–95
Buzz-Saw Blues exercise, 21

## C

Caccini, Giulio, 231–233
Caffeine, 38
Caird, John, 201–207

Calloway, Cab, 125–127
*Carousel* (play), 189–194
*Cats* (play), 194–198
Chest cavity, 7, 8*f*, 9
Chest register, 15
Christmas, 68–71, 226–231, 289–290
Classical music, 231–278
Cocker, Joe, 147–151
Cohan, George M., 100–102, 106–116,
    160–164
Color, of voice, 33–34
Colored pencil, 31
*Con Air* (film), 122–125
Consonants, 5
Cornelius, Peter, 246–249
Coughing, 38
Cracking voice, 30
Cricoid cartilage, 12, 13*f*, 14
Cue card, 32
Cumulative method, 32

## D

Darion, Joe, 181–185
d'Hardelot, Guy, 76–80
Diaphragm
    physiology of, 7, 8*f*, 9
    seated posture and, 24
Dion, Celine, 127–137, 312–320
*Don Juan DeMarco* (film), 116–121
Down the Stairs exercise, 19
Duets, 40, 293–328
Duration, of practice, 24–25

## E

Emmett, Dan D., 80–82
Emotions, 33–36
Epiglottis, 12, 13*f*, 14
Esophagus, 14
Exercises
    for breath support, 10–11
    for care of voice, 39
    vocalizing, 17–21
Exhaling
    breath support exercises and, 10–11
    physiology of, 7, 8, 9
External intercostal muscles, 8
External oblique muscles, 8
Eyes, 35

## F

Facial expressions, 35, 36
Falsetto, 16
Fatigue, 27, 37
*Fiddler on the Roof* (play), 173–181
*Figaro* (opera), 274–278
Fisher, Bruce, 147–151
Foster, David, 312–320
Foster, Stephen C., 72–75, 86–91
Franklin, Aretha, 138–142

## G

Gargling, 39
Germany, 289–290
Gershwin, George, 217–226
Gershwin, Ira, 217–226
Gestures, 35–36
Graham, Brendan, 151–157
Groban, Josh, 151–157

## H

"Hail Mary" (prayer), 49–56
Hammerstein, Oscar III, 168–173,
    189–194, 198–201, 212–217,
    308–312
Hand movements, 35–36
Hanukkah, 65–66
Harburg, E. Y., 207–212
Harman, Jerry, 226–231
Harnick, Sheldon, 173–181
Hart, Lorenz, 198–201
Hawaiian music, 82–86
Head position, 2
Head register, 15, 20–21
Head Register/Breath Support
    A-Go-Go exercise, 20–21
Heise, P., 255–256
Heyward, Dorothy, 222–226
Heyward, Du Bose, 222–226
High notes, 30
Hissing, 10
Horner, James, 127–137
Humming exercise, 18
Hyoid bone, 12, 13*f*, 14

## I

Illness, 38
Improvement, 27
Inflection, 5

Inhaling
  breath support exercises and, 10–11
  physiology of, 7, 8, 9
Intercostal muscles, 8
Internal intercostal muscles, 8
Internal oblique muscles, 8
International songs, 279–292
Ireland, 284–285
Italy, 280–282

**J**
Jaw tension, 20

**K**
Kamen, Michael, 116–121
Kaplan, Abraham, 61–64
Kennedy, Amanda, 68–71
Kern, Philip, 42–49
*Kiss Me, Kate* (play), 320–328
Kittredge, Walter, 104–106
Koehler, Chas, 93–95
Kretzmer, Herbert, 201–207, 257–260

**L**
Language, 5
Laryngopharynx, 15
Larynx, 12–14, 15
Laughing exercise, 10–11
Learning music, 4–6, 30–32
Legato vocal line, 5
Leigh, Mitch, 181–185
Lent, 56
*Les Miserables* (play), 157–160,
  201–207
Listening, to self, 3, 35
*Little Johnny Jones* (play), 160–164
Løvland, Rolf, 151–157
Lungs, 7, 8f, 9

**M**
MacDowell, Edward A., 272–274
*The Magic Flute* (opera), 242–244
Male voice, 16
*Mame* (play), 226–231
*Man of La Mancha* (play), 181–185
Mask, 15
Medicines, 38
Melodies, 4–5
Memorization, 31–32
Middle register, 15
Mills, Irving, 125–127
Mirror exercises, 35
Morning exercises, 17, 18
Morse, Theodore, 96–99
Mouth, 15, 19
Mozart, W. A., 242–244, 274–278
Muscles, 7–8
Music
  learning of, 4–6, 30–32
  making of, 33–36
*The Music Man* (play), 164–168

**N**
Nasopharynx, 15
Natel, Jean-Marc, 201–207
Nervousness, 31
No Jaw Tension Hoedown exercise, 20
Nodules, 37
Nonmusical sounds, 34
Nose, 15
Nunn, Trevor, 194–198, 201–207

**O**
Offenbach, Jacques, 233–238
*Oh, Kay!* (play), 217–222
O'Hara, Geoffrey, 56–61
*Oklahoma!* (play), 168–173, 308–312
Oldies, 72–116
Oropharynx, 15

**P**
Pain, 27
Patriotic songs, 91–92, 100–116
Pencil, 31
Penn, Arthur A., 102–104
Performance
  facial expressions and, 35
  gestures and, 35–36
  music learning before, 30–32
  overview of, 33
  timbres and, 33–34
Pergolesi, G. B., 264–266
*Phantom of the Opera* (play),
  293–298
Pharynx, 15
Phonation, 12
Physical sensations
  overview of, 3
  technique assessment and, 27
  vocalizing and, 21
Piano, 4, 11, 23
Pitch, 18, 19
Plan, practice, 22–23
Poetry, 34
Polyps, 37
Popular music, 116–157
*Porgy and Bess* (play), 222–226
Porter, Cole, 320–328
Posture
  for breath support, 11
  care of voice and, 37
  practice and, 22, 23
  of singer's stance, 1–3
  song performance and, 36
  for vocalizing exercises, 17
Practice, 22–25, 27, 36
Preston, Billy, 147–151
Psalms, 61–64
Punctuation, 30

**R**
Reading music, 4–6
Recorder, 4, 23

Rectus abdominus, 8
Redding, Otis, 138–142
Register
  anatomy and, 15–16
  exercises with, 20–21
  overview of, 15
Rehearsal, 22
Repetition, 31–32
Resonance, 14–15
Resonator, 14
Respiratory system, 7–8
Rest, 39
Rhythm, 4
Rib cage, 8, 24
Rodgers, Richard, 168–173, 189–194,
  198–201, 212–217, 308–312

**S**
Sacred music, 41–71
Sager, Carole Bayer, 312–320
Salt water gargling, 39
Scales, 10, 19–20
Scarlatti, A., 251–255
Schönberg, Claude-Michel, 157–160,
  201–207, 257–260
Schubert, Franz, 49–56
Score mapping, 30–31
Scotland, 285–287
Scott, Sir Walter, 49
Screaming, 38
Seated posture, 23–24
Sensations
  overview of, 3
  technique assessment and, 27
  vocalizing and, 21
Shoulder position, 2
Sigh-Slide exercise, 18
Singer's stance, 2–3, 22
Sinus, 15
Siren-Slide exercise, 18
Skipping Up-and-Down the Stairs
  exercise, 19–20
Sleeping, 39
Smiling, 35
Smoking, 38
Sondheim, Stephen, 185–189
Song anthology, 40. *See also Song
  index*
Sound production, 12–16
*South Pacific* (play), 212–217
Spain, 282–284, 287–289, 290–292
Speaking voice, 1, 12–16, 18
Stage fright, 31
Stage music, 157–231, 293–312
Stance, 2–3
*Sweeney Todd* (play), 185–189

**T**
*The Tales of Hoffman* (opera),
  233–238
Tchaikovsky, P., 266–272

Teacher, 3, 21
Technique, 26–27
Tempo, 4
Text, of song, 5–6, 34
Thiele, Bob, 143–147
Thyro-arytenoid muscle, 13
Thyroid cartilage, 12, 13*f*, 14
Timbre, 33–34
Time, practice, 24–25
Tired voice, 27
*Titanic* (film), 127–137
Tongue, 19
Tonic triad, 17
Tosti, F. Paolo, 256–261
Trachea, 7, 8*f*, 12, 14

**U**
Up-and-Down the Stairs exercise, 19

**V**
Vacuum, 9
Vandersloot, F. W., 82–86
Verbal repetition, 32
Vocal folds, 12–13
Vocal register. *See* Register
Vocal rest, 39
Vocal technique, 26–27
Vocalizing, 17–21
Voice
   care of, 37–39
   color of, 33–34
Voice box, 12–14
Voice classes, 1
Vowels
   breath support and, 10
   vocalizations with, 17, 19
   in words of songs, 5

**W**
Wales, 279–280
Warren, Diane, 122–125
Water intake, 39
Webber, Andrew Lloyd, 194–198,
   293–298
Wedding music, 76–80,
   312–320
Weiss, George David, 143–147
Whispering, 38
Willson, Meredith, 164–167
*The Wizard of Oz* (play), 207–212
Words, of songs, 5–6, 34
Writing repetition, 31

**Y**
Yearwood, Trisha, 122–125
Yelling, 38